HIGHWAY ROBBERY

HIGHWAY

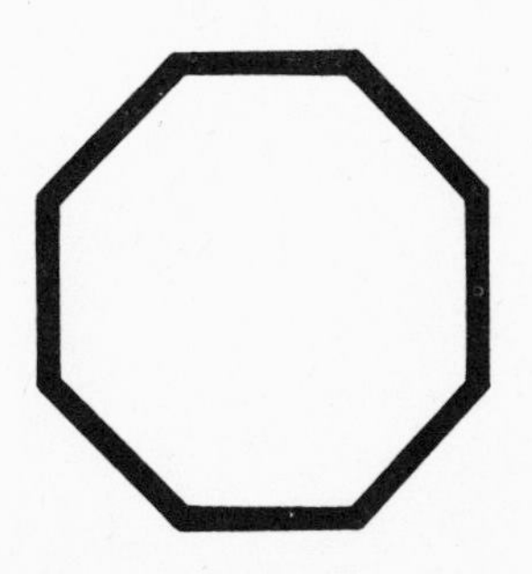

ROBBERY

Sam Crowther

AND

Irwin Winehouse

STEIN AND DAY/*Publishers*/New York

Library of Congress Catalog Card No. 66-14947

Published simultaneously in Canada by Saunders of Toronto, Ltd.

DESIGNED BY BERNARD SCHLEIFER
Manufactured in the United States of America

Stein and Day / *Publishers* / 7 E. 48 St., New York, N. Y. 10017

THIRD PRINTING

THIS BOOK is dedicated to the women in our lives—
those who lived through the writing of it,
Jean Crowther and Angelina Winehouse; and
those who worked untiringly and unstintingly with us,
Louise Bach, Mary Jean Alleva, and Claire LeJuez

Foreword

THIS IS an important book which makes intriguing reading but sad living.

It involves everyone who rides in an automobile—owners and passengers of the 82,000,000 cars which are such an integral, basic part of our living pattern. And the problems discussed in this book are not confined to the United States: they're worldwide.

I can vouch for this book because I was part of it. Many of the disclosures are the results of investigations by my office when I was the District Attorney of Queens County in New York City.

Members of my staff and I worked closely with the co-author of HIGHWAY ROBBERY, reporter Sam Crowther. As a result of one probe—into the widespread operations of gyp mechanics—Mr. Crowther received the coveted Wilbur Finley Fawley Prize ("for outstanding public service") from the Columbia Graduate School of Journalism.

Since then, my office has further aided Mr. Crowther and Irwin Winehouse in developing material for this much needed, long-overdue book. Extensive reports and case histories from our files were made available to the authors.

Now, at last, they have spoken out, citing chapter and verse of the almost unbelievable story of the multibillion dollar swindle being perpetrated against the American motoring public.

The revelations may shock you. But that is the purpose of this daring book—to wake us all up. Too long has the car owner suffered abuse silently, without access to legal protection and redress.

As one who has been concerned with the problems of law enforcement for over 25 years, I firmly believe that the time has come to institute safeguards for the motorist on a city, state and federal level. Strong, realistic legislation, properly and vigorously enforced, can help assure America's car owners a square deal. No law can protect a gullible or undemanding or timid public indefinitely. But legislation and enforcement will not be enough. The public must be constantly on the alert to help protect itself.

HIGHWAY ROBBERY should be read and remembered.

Frank D. O'Connor
President, City Council
New York, N.Y.

Acknowledgments

WE WISH TO ACKNOWLEDGE the help of some of the organizations and people who supplied both guidance and assistance in the development of this book. Without their support and the information they were willing to make available to us, this book could never have been written:

Paul H. Douglas, U.S. Senator from Illinois, and his assistant, Jonathan Lindley;

Frank D. O'Connor, President, New York City Council, former District Attorney, Queens County, New York;

James F. O'Donnell, Confidential Assistant, Queens County (N.Y.) District Attorney's office; Francis X. Smith, Assistant District Attorney and Chief of the Rackets Bureau, Queens County; and Gordon O'Neill, Detective Investigator;

J. Carroll Bateman, General Manager, and John Loser, Director of Press Relations, Insurance Information Institute;

Hugh R. Jackson, Andrew Duffy and L. C. Troise, Better Business Bureau of New York City;

James D. Horan, Assistant Managing Editor, and Don Frasca, Sunday City Editor, *The Journal-American;*

Milton Machlin, Managing Editor, *Argosy* magazine;

Louis J. Lefkowitz, Attorney General, State of New York;

William Eckhoff, Public Relations Director, New York State Motor Vehicle Bureau;

Edward J. Speno, New York State Senator, former Chairman, Joint Legislative Committee of Motor Vehicles and Traffic Safety;

James P. Economos, Director of Traffic Court Programs, American Bar Association, Chicago, Illinois;

Paul Rand Dixon, Chairman, Federal Trade Commission;

Virgil W. Peterson, Operating Director, Chicago Crime Commission;

John di Lorenzi, Public Relations Director, and Cornelius R. "Hap" Gray, Director Legal Department, American Automobile Association;

Detective Sergeant Hubert R. McKenna, Commanding Officer, Auto Squad, New York City Police Department;

Morgan Woods, Chief, Claims Department, and Robert W. Dick, Assistant Claims Manager, American Insurance Association;

Bernard J. O'Connell, former New York City License Commissioner, and his associate, Joseph Di Carlo;

William Davidson, Director of Information, New York State Thruway;

John J. O'Brien, President and General Manager, Better Business Bureau of Greater St. Louis;

Maurice E. Trimmer, Press Secretary to the Governor, State of New Mexico;

A. Ridgely Jones, Vice-President, Pensacola, Fla., Motor Club;

Federal Bureau of Investigation, Washington, D.C., Chicago, and New York;

National Commission on Safety Education, National Education Association;

Consumers Union and *Consumer Reports;*

And last, but not least, we must thank the many informants who gave us leads as well as detailed case-histories. Though they must remain anonymous, we are grateful for their help.

The Authors

Contents

HIGHWAY ROBBERY

Introduction

Misled. Tricked. Robbed. Swindled. Victimized.

Any or all of these terms can properly be applied to that abused citizen—the American motorist. He is today being taken, through a combination of his own ignorance and others' chicanery, for over *seven billion* dollars a year. And, in many instances, he is totally ignorant of having been hoodwinked.

America's car owners—82,000,000 of them—are a beaten and bewildered lot. They are swindled by mechanics in a racket that has now reached $100,000,000-a-year proportions. They are the dupes of used-car merchants and of new-car dealers alike.

On the highways of this land, they are deliberately led into speed traps, deceived by tow-car rackets, overcharged by trickery in the rent-a-car field, and forced to seek highway justice before officers of the court whose income, in many cases, is actually based upon the amount of fines collected.

Most seriously, when a tire explodes on a turnpike and a motorist loses his life—who is there to point the finger of accusation at those who have fought against every attempt to enable the driver to buy safe tires by standardizing tire quality?

In food and drugs, airline and rail transportation, banking and finance, to name but a few sensitive areas of consumer interest, an attempt is made to protect the public. But in the automobile field—the hub of industrial America—the accepted attitude is one of the-public-be-damned, and abuse is standard.

Detroit car manufacturers give every new-car dealer an allowance (between $50 and $100) to perform a final inspection before each new car leaves a showroom. But how many dealers—or should one say how few—ever earn that allowance?

In most states, one needs a license to practice barbering, but not to do clipping as an auto mechanic. Charging a customer for a set of spark plugs that were never installed can, at worst, result in a complaint that finds its way into the American Automobile Association or Better Business Bureau files—and languishes there.

When one of us launched an exposé of the car-repair racket with a series of articles in the *New York Journal-American,* the story brought over 2,000 letters from irate car owners detailing their own sad experiences. Each had been taken, but none had found any redress except to tell his story to a newspaperman in the hopes that the harsh light of publicity would bring corrective measures.

The public be damned? In one state, the Park Department found itself unable to award a franchise for towing on state highways. No company wanted the job since the state had not only set fair towing charges—$4.00 for the first mile and $1.00 per mile thereafter—but insisted that the towing company be *independent of any garage.* The rule: No fleecing of motorists on repairs simply because one had physical possession of his car. And, so, no takers. Finally, the state was forced to relent. Cars would be towed, at the fixed rate, to any garage, including one owned by the tow-car company.

Ignorance plays a large role in continued abuse. Motorists are too-easy victims of misleading advertising. Most drivers, particularly women, do not understand the inner workings of a car and can be told, or sold, anything. Almost everyone is confused by the details of automobile financing, and no one knows where to report an overcharge or a false advertising claim and hope to have anything done about it.

Clearly, the problem is too big for the motorist to handle himself. The entire field needs full investigation and, ultimately, some form of supervision. First, however, must come the facts, the detailed report of case after case to show how thievery is conducted and the motorist is defrauded.

It is the purpose of this book to bring to the attention of both the motorist and civic official the widespread nature of malpractice. From this, hopefully, may come some restraint of multi-million dollar rackets that flourish under the umbrella of the law.

An informed and angered public will demand action, we are certain. This nation's people do not look kindly on being made fools of. Inequities have always made American blood boil and brought a clamor for justice.

Here, then, is the full story of the highway robbery in this country—the facts about how car owners are being swindled every hour of every day.

CHAPTER I

New cars: how you'll get used

IN THE SUBURBS of New York's Westchester County, Sylvia and Dave Edwards were a one-car family in two-car surroundings. The Edwards weren't status-conscious, but with the arrival of their fifth child they became space conscious: it was time to trade in their sedan for a station wagon.

Dave drove over to a nearby dealer whose much publicized slogan was: "No deal turned down. All we want are satisfied customers." He was greeted by a salesman who was happy to introduce himself as Lou—and very happy indeed to introduce Dave to just the new station wagon he wanted. "Okay," said Dave, "now what kind of a deal can you give me?"

Lou went out, took a look at the Edwards' sedan, did some rapid calculating, and told them: "You can have this station wagon for your old car plus $1,900." Dave agreed eagerly enough. He was ushered into a small office and there signed a contract. The station wagon would be delivered in three weeks.

Two days later a telephone call came from the dealer's sales manager: "Mr. Edwards," he said, "your car has been reappraised. We found a lot of trouble in the transmission. The way it stands it doesn't have much of a market value. We'll have to charge you $200 more."

"But I've already signed a contract for $1,900," Dave insisted, "and I expect you to stick by it."

"Which salesman made the agreement with you?" the sales manager asked.

"His name was Lou something."

"You mean Russell? We got rid of him! He was writing contracts which were not in accord with company policy."

Ultimately Dave bought his new station wagon at the revised price. He never knew he had been a victim of what is known in the trade as the "highball" racket. This trick is employed when a customer buys a new car with a trade-in. First, there is the phony price agreed to at the signing of the contract. Then there is always the upgraded price before actual delivery of the new car.

A spokesman for the Better Business Bureau explains: "Most people don't know that an automobile salesman is not an officer of the company. His signature on a contract is not binding. On the other hand, the buyer's signature is. Therefore, the automobile agency has the option of backing out of the contract at its own discretion. In most cases the victim doesn't realize what is happening to him. Highballing exists in most metropolitan areas throughout the country. We know this from reports we receive from other bureaus."

Filed complaints to the BBB are endless: "I went into a contract with a dealer who stated that he would deliver a new, custom two-door sedan for $2,000 in trade for my five-year-old Ford. The Ford was inspected by the salesman, who quoted a price. I left a deposit and was assured of delivery."

A few days later the Ford owner got a phone call from the salesman.

"I'm in a real bind on your deal because the boss didn't okay the contract."

"Why not?"

"I figured too high on your old car," the salesman replied, putting personal unhappiness into his voice.

"What's that got to do with me? We made a deal."

"It's not that simple. The boss says the price on the new car will have to be upped by $215. He says he didn't sign any contract so legally it's no deal."

The Ford owner finally paid but, after filing a complaint, he told investigators, "I only paid to avoid the aggravation of haggling."

Another case, from the Midwest: "I ordered a new car after we came to an agreement on price and trade-in allowance. I signed the agreement and they told me I could pick up my new car in four weeks. When I came back a month later with a bank check, I was told the manager would have to look over my old car. He did. Then he said the salesman who had sold me the car had acted without his approval. An additional $200 was added to the original agreement."

A variation, this time from the South: "My wife and I visited a showroom. The salesman showed us a car which he described as having a 'modified Thunderbird' engine. He said it also had two-speed washer-wipers. It sounded good and I arranged with him to buy the car with that equipment. When I showed up for delivery, I discovered that the engine was not the special 'Thunderbird,' and that there were no washer-wipers on the car. Believe it or not, they told me the salesman had simply forgotten to write these in on the order. The equipment could not, therefore, be included at the agreed-upon price. Rather than wait, I paid."

This complaint came from a woman: "I bought a new car and had trouble with the radio. When I brought it in for service I was told the radio was not the original equipment and I'd have to pay $15 to have it fixed. This was ridiculous—I'd only had the car for a few months. I complained to the sales manager that he was using cheap and illegal tactics and showed him my new-car warranty. He got angry and said that the price to fix the radio was now $25. Then he shouted, 'The more trouble you cause, the higher the charge will be.' "

And from California: "I signed a trade-in contract after my old car was inspected by the dealer and accepted. I drove off with the new one and left the other.

A few days later, I received a telephone call and was told, 'Your trade-in car has a cracked windshield. The shock absorbers and the brakes are not in good condition. We had to put an additional $145 on your finance contract.' "

And so the highballing rolls on.

New-car buyers who aren't cheated in this particular way may instead find themselves victims of a practice known as "loading the deal." A customer will order what's described to him as a "standard" car. But when he calls to take delivery, he finds that the "standard" car he wanted is not available and will not be "for quite some time." The salesman usually goes on to explain that the model which *was* delivered from the factory is one with a number of extras.

"What do you mean 'extras'?" the customer asks.

"The factory included some things you didn't ask for."

"Like what?"

"Well, this car has power steering, power brakes, a padded dash, heavy-duty battery, push-button radio, two-speed windshield wipers, and back-up lights."

"But all I wanted was a standard car. How much would the extras cost me?"

"Well, since you'd be getting them at cost, your monthly payments would only be increased by a small amount," the salesman explains.

What the buyer did not take pencil, paper and time to figure out was that he was buying almost $300 worth of equipment which he hadn't asked for and didn't want, yet which had been slyly loaded onto the original price he agreed to.

Example, Chicago: "I ordered a new car for $3,200. When it arrived it was loaded with extra equipment. I was told there had been a mix-up at the factory and that the extras would cost me another $325. I didn't want to wait for another car so I paid it."

Atlanta: "I ordered a new car with standard equipment. When it finally arrived, I was told there would be an additional charge of $424 for air conditioning. I insisted that I hadn't ordered air conditioning and they said: 'Everybody in the South wants air conditioning these days so we assumed you did too.' When I still said no, they told me: 'Deliveries are very slow now—you'll probably have to wait three months for another car.' "

Los Angeles: "I ordered air conditioning with my new car. When it arrived, there was an extra charge for a tinted windshield. I was told: 'You have to have a tinted windshield with air conditioning.' I'm still trying to find out why."

In the area of optional equipment there is the reverse twist: not getting what you ordered, or getting equipment inferior to that which you paid for. Cases in point:

"I ordered a compact car and specified heavy-duty shock absorbers and a heavy-duty radiator as I go camping a good deal and have to carry heavy equipment. When I got the car, the shocks didn't seem stiff enough. I had the car checked, and found that both the shocks and the radiator were standard—although I had ordered and paid for heavy-duty items."

And: "On my order, I specified a deluxe push-button radio that cost me $63. Not long after taking delivery of the automobile I had some trouble with the radio's reception and took it to a repair shop. The repairman looked at the radio and then at me. 'You're another one!' he said. I asked him what he meant, and he told me I didn't have a factory-installed radio at all, but a cheap Japanese model which had been substituted somewhere along the line."

In another instance, a woman ordered undercoating because her service station man had told her it would add two years to the life of her car. Some weeks later she took the car to the service station for an oil change and grease job. When she returned to pick up the car, it was still on the rack. The service station man came over and commented: "It's a nice car, but I told you to have it undercoated, didn't I?"

Without his casual remark, the woman might never have discovered that she had been cheated of the $50 she paid for undercoating.

Now we shift to what the trade calls "make ready," more formally known as "New Car Pre-Delivery Inspection and Adjustment Check-Up." The manufacturer gives the dealer an allowance of between $50 and $100, depending on the kind of car, to make this final check after a car has been delivered from the factory and before it is turned over to a customer.

The objective is to spot and correct irregularities which may have been missed during factory inspection. But unscrupulous dealers pocket this make-ready allowance and trust to luck the factory inspection caught everything. They perform the make-ready service only if the customer returns with a complaint—and sometimes not even then.

Most new-car owners look forward to having a trouble-free car. When something minor seems wrong, they often don't feel they can afford to take time to bring the car back to the dealer's—they only do this when confronted with a major breakdown. Having a new car laid up in a crowded waiting line at a dealer's garage works enough of a hardship on owners that they go instead for the quicker attention of the nearest service station.

These are typical cases, taken from the files of investigative agencies around the country:

Seattle musician: "I complained to the dealer that there was something wrong with the transmission, and he said the trouble would be taken care of at the 1,000-mile check-up. When I took the car in I was told a 'valve' was missing and that the particular part had been back-ordered. I waited a whole week before going back for my car. It was still being worked on—they said the transmission needed a band adjustment. A few days later I picked up the car and found the transmission still causing the same trouble. But then, since I had waited for the 1,000-mile check-up, I was faced with the possibility of the car's breaking down after the warranty had expired."

Brooklyn subway motorman: "I took my new car back for some adjustments—fast idle, defective horn, defective trunk lock, loose parking brake and a few other things. The salesman told me I would have to leave the car over the weekend. They loaned me an old car to use in the meanwhile.

"Monday I went to pick up my car. There was a 24-inch scratch on the right side and the gas tank was almost empty. Inside, the ashtrays were full of cigarette butts. When I complained to the manager, he acted as if it was nothing unusual and said casually that the salesman had taken the car home for the weekend."

Fort Lee, New Jersey, housewife: "The car cost me $2,700 but I haven't had one bit of enjoyment from it. The front door on the driver's side springs open. I went back to complain a number of times. I would talk to the dealer and then would be shifted to a mechanic. They kept passing the buck. One mechanic told me, 'The car should never have left the factory in that condition.' When I told the dealer what the mechanic said, he couldn't have been less interested."

Midland, Michigan, surgeon: "I have owned several automobiles in the past and have always received courteous and considerate treatment. Maybe I was spoiled.

The last car I bought was supposed to be undercoated and porcelainized. They did neither. I was told by the manager to bring the car back and it would be taken care of. I did. Still nothing done. Excuses. No time. I was told it would be done during the 1,000-mile check-up, but it wasn't. There were a number of other things that weren't taken care of—the wipers were not adjusted, wheels weren't balanced and grease spots on the roof were not removed.

"Only then did I discover that there were a number of complaints against the same dealer. What could I do? I wrote to the manufacturer, but the same dealer is still handling his cars and all I received for my troubles was a neatly typed letter from Detroit."

St. Louis housewife: "There were a number of things wrong with my car which the dealer said would be corrected when I brought it in for the 1,000-mile oil change. We had had a rain storm and the car leaked around both the windshield and the top of the door. When I got the car back, the dealer said the leak had been corrected. A few days later it rained again. This time, the windshield leaked so badly that the floors, both front and back, were dripping wet."

Mobile, Alabama, beautician: "The car I bought may be a credit to the manufacturer, but I can't say the same about the dealer. It took me three separate visits to get the gas gauge working. The first time I took the car in they replaced the gauge, the second time they replaced the unit on the dash, and on the third trip they put in a

CHAPTER II

Used cars: well-worn tricks

THE HORSE TRADER is an established part of the American tradition. At any turn-of-century horse sale, he was quick to spot, among a crowd of farmers, an obvious city man—a would-be gentleman farmer. An easy mark for the wily trader, the gentleman would soon find himself the owner of a mare whose step seemed sprightly and whose coat was a gleaming black.

Once back at his farm, the city man was likely to find that his new animal, on a farmhand's inspection, turned out to be debilitated. She was not black at all, but gray—a coat of shoe black had been applied to the poor beast. There was the distinct smell of whiskey on her breath, administered to keep her looking alive. And her teeth had been filed down to belie her real age.

Crooked horse-trading pretty much ended with the advent of the automobile. But the techniques of trickery were simply transferred—to used-car salesmen. Nothing changed but the merchandise. Says a spokesman for the National Better Business Bureau:

"The sale of used cars constitutes one of the largest single sources of complaints received by Better Business Bureaus around the country. It would be impossible to give even a rough estimate of the extent of the victimization. Consider the fact that two used cars are sold for every new one. Yet the complaints on used cars are three to one."

Here's one such complaint from Chicago, Illinois: "I bought a three-year-old sedan and was told it was in perfect condition. The salesman said it had just been given a factory paint job. I started on a trip to Cleveland. On the ramp to the Turnpike the transmission went out. I had to pay to have the car towed back to the dealer. While I was waiting for the service manager, I started to look over the car more closely. I noticed there were spots where the paint was already starting to peel. Maybe I shouldn't use the word paint. It looked more like shoe polish."

Brooklyn, New York: "I contracted for a 1958 station wagon after seeing an ad for a 'Giant Auto Sale.' A salesman told me he had just the car for me. It was this 1958 station wagon on which I made a deposit of $250. After I had signed the contract and they had my money,

I found that the car had a cracked block. I asked my insurance company to have someone look the car over. They sent a representative who checked and said the car was not fit for the road. Only after I threatened to call the police was I finally able to get my money back."

Some sharp traders even claim to be "helping the poor."

An expensively dressed lawyer for a used-car dealer went to the headquarters of the Better Business Bureau in New York City recently to lodge this complaint with a staff member:

"What are you trying to do to my client? You're telling people he's some kind of crook."

"All we can tell you," said the staff member, "is that your client's operation has resulted in an enormous number of complaints filed with this office."

"My client," the lawyer explained, "conducts his business as part of the anti-poverty program. I handle the financing for him. You see, our market is among the low-income groups, Negroes and Puerto Ricans. The only requirement made for credit is that the buyer have a job."

"Even if he has a garnishee on his salary?"

"That is correct."

"How are you able to operate a lending service where the credit risks are so poor?"

"We have faith in people. The regular finance companies are too strict. We help the poor."

"What do you get out of it?"

"I buy the paper."

"At what discount?"

"Forty per cent."

The BBB probed further into the operation to determine how the dealer was able to factor the loan at such a high discount rate. The answer proved to be quite simple. The cost of high discounting was made up by selling used cars to poor people at prices far above the market value and repossessing the cars at the slightest delay in meeting payments.

Guarantees which turn out not to be guarantees but simply come-ons are among the biggest sources of complaint. Pick up any newspaper and notice the scores of used-car ads with the line: "All Cars Guaranteed." The impression given is that if anything goes wrong, the car need merely be returned to the dealer for prompt free-of-charge repair. This isn't the case at all.

Actually, many used cars are sold on a "50-50 30-day" guarantee. This means that if a defect develops during the first thirty days of ownership, the dealer will pay half the cost of all repairs. In most cases, the dealer tries to wriggle out of the guarantee by stalling the owner beyond the 30-day period. If he does make the repairs, the customer, instead of getting the usual discount, is always charged full list price for everything. Thus the car owner ends up paying about the same as he would have without the "guarantee."

A complaint from Mineola, Long Island: "I bought a sports car and began to have trouble right away. The generator wasn't charging. I had to have the battery charged twice and on four occasions had to be pushed to get started. I took the car back twice but was told by the service manager that it would be several weeks before they could get to the car. They were trying to stall until the 30-day warranty ran out. I had the car looked over by a mechanic. In addition to the generator the following things were wrong: brakes out of adjustment, leaky fuel pump, doors hard to lock, knock in motor, no parking lights and worn hood latch. Yet I had been given an 'A-1 Performance Protection Policy'!"

Yonkers, N. Y.: "I left a deposit on a 1959 hardtop. But when I went back to the lot, after my credit had been approved, I was told that the car had been sold. They offered me a four-door sedan which I refused, but I finally agreed to buy a convertible as a substitute. I started on a trip from New York on the New Jersey Turnpike. The motor just stopped. I had to have the car towed off the turnpike and back to New York. The dealer refused to pay the charge even though I had a guarantee. They've had the car now for three weeks and I still haven't heard what is going to happen."

Philadelphia, Pa.: "I owned a Thunderbird and owed a balance of $2,600. I told them I wanted to get a Cadillac but I didn't have enough money for a down payment. They told me they would lend me an automobile while I was making up my mind. The car was a Chrysler. I signed some papers which I thought had to do with using the car temporarily. Then, I found out I had signed to buy the Chrysler. After I had a heart attack and was unable to continue payments, they repossessed the car and said I owed them $2,126.38."

St. Louis, Mo.: Bob Drew saw an ad offering year-old Fords for $1,095. The ad said the cars were in excellent condition and had been driven "comparatively little."

Bob found only one car on the lot at the advertised price. "You wouldn't want that clunker," the salesman said. "But this bargain over here, for $1,800, is a real steal." Drew insisted on the advertised car, and finally it was sold to him—without a receipt and only after a long and heated argument.

Bob Drew, actually an investigator for the BBB, had the car towed to an authorized mechanic for examination.

There was an offensive smell when the car's doors were open. The front seats had no supports. Padding oozed from great gashes in the upholstery. Motor parts were disconnected or entirely missing. Papers found in the car verified the mechanic's opinion that it was a "clunker"; in fact, it was a ruined police cruiser.

The dealer had spent good money to advertise a clunker he didn't want to sell—merely as bait to lure poor fish.

It is a widespread practice to advertise cars on a "take over payments" basis. The pitch is that the original owner was unable to meet monthly charges. A report turned in by a shopper for the Better Business Bureau reads:

"I followed up an ad for a Chevrolet Power-Glide at $50-a-month for 24 months. At the car lot, I was told the Chevy had been sold. The salesman showed me another car: it was a three-year-old sedan, yet the speedometer read only 13,000 miles. I asked if I could have the car checked over by my own mechanic. The salesman refused."

(In a complaint against this same dealer, the prospective customer was persuaded to leave his registration paper in lieu of a down-payment. He returned the same day, having decided against buying a car, but the salesman refused to return his registration. Only after he complained to the BBB did he finally get it back.)

There can be no clear-cut set of *Do's* and *Don'ts* for buying a used car. But over the years the Better Business Bureau has developed some general rules which, while they won't eliminate the possibility of your getting stuck with a lemon, will cut down on that likelihood.

Most importantly, try to *have a mechanic you know check the things you don't have the ability to check.*

General appearance

External appearance is not conclusive, but it can give you some idea of a car's previous use and care. An owner who has neglected the cleanliness and appearance of his car may also have neglected mechanical parts.

Look at the upholstery, under the seat covers, for extent of wear. Examine convertible tops. Make sure that they operate properly, and watch for tears. The driver's seat, the front floor boards, and foot pedals may give you an idea of the extent and kind of wear a car has had. Door catches can also be informative.

Minor dents or repairs in used car fenders are not

necessarily a danger signal. But if you suspect the fenders have been seriously damaged, examine the undersides. A new fender could mean the car had been in a serious accident, or that the original fender had been damaged beyond repair.

Trial driving

Most owner complaints about used cars come from people who didn't actually drive the cars before buying them. *If the dealer won't let you drive a car, don't buy it.* Reputable dealers expect to be in business a long time and are eager to have you drive before you buy.

For a trial drive, the engine should be allowed to warm up. If the car doesn't have an automatic shift, try the clutch—jerky starting may mean the clutch is worn. The clutch should not slip when the motor is speeded up.

If you can't idle the car to a slow speed, ask why. It may indicate mechanical trouble or improper adjustment.

Does the car drive easily? Is there too much play in the steering wheel, or kickback or wobble in the front wheels? Is there any gear-grinding noise?

Check the brakes by applying them suddenly. Note whether the wheels brake evenly. Get out and examine the skid marks. (Better still, have the brakes tested on a brake-testing machine.) Try the emergency or parking brake on a steep hill to see if it holds the car.

Drive the car up a steep hill, or try a fast get-away

into high speed from a dead stop. Does the motor pull easily and quietly?

Check the speedometer (or, to be technically correct, the odometer, which registers mileage). As will be discussed in Chapter III, it's general practice with many used-car dealers to set odometers back. So check the reading against the general condition of the car. If the car registers 12,000 miles and you're told it was owned by a retired minister who drove it only 10 miles a week —but the car has brand-new tires, look out. The odds are ten-to-one it was driven a good deal more than 12,000 miles by someone other than a retired minister. Note the arm rests and gas pedal. Are they worn to a greater degree than the mileage indicates? Remember that it takes plenty of driving to wear down pedal pads and arm rests.

Exhaust

In checking a used car, if you notice an excessive amount of smoke coming from the exhaust when you speed up or slow down—stop. This is a danger signal. If it persists, it usually means the car is burning oil and needs a complete engine overhaul. Walk away from this one.

Used taxicabs

Cabs, generally subjected to long mileage and hard usage, are usually not good buys. *The average cab in a metropolitan area does 100,000 miles in a single year.* Fly-by-night dealers will re-paint taxis and misrepresent them as cars previously owned by private persons. Be on the watch: almost all taxis are four door sedans; most can be detected by their special style and fittings. The former insignia may show through the paint. Look for indentations in the metal where taxi lights or signs might once have been placed. Open doors and see if edges reveal an undercoat of a common taxi color. Look for excessive wear on bumpers, edges of hood, running boards and fenders. A used taxi will ride hard; the transmission and rear end is noisy; the brakes are hard; the motor has lost its life, and will handle heavily. Finally, a check of the motor or serial number through license records can tell you if the used car is an ex-cab.

The dealer

To find out about his reliability, ask your local Better Business Bureau if it has any complaints against the dealer you plan to use. It may cost you more to buy from a reputable dealer. But it's dollars well spent if he himself has spent time and money to put the car you want in good condition. If a dealer offers prices well below those of others in the neighborhood—watch out. If you look for and find a "real beauty at an unbelievable price"—you're being taken.

Perfection should not be expected in a used car. Be prepared for some wear and tear. If a car is described as "reconditioned," the dependable dealer will show you in what way it has been reconditioned.

In those states where inspection of motor vehicles is required, the dealer should either provide the necessary inspection certificate himself or guarantee in writing that the car will pass such inspection.

Insist on a detailed, receipted bill covering the facts about your purchase. The guarantee on your car, if you are promised one, should also be given to you at the time you pay. Without this document, you have no redress. If the car is a financed purchase, insist that the papers be made out *before* you sign them, and get the copy you are entitled to.

And finally, though it may sound like an unnecessary warning, never sign *anything* before you have carefully read *all* the papers involved in a transaction.

CHAPTER III

Doctored cars: surgery for swindle

BILL FENTON lived in the Queens section of New York City, worked hard at his job, and dreamed of buying a new car for a vacation trip to Florida. He and his wife Alma skimped until finally they had enough for a down payment. But they were unsure of where to go to get the most for their money. Then they heard of a dealer who advertised himself on the radio and in print as "Tony Discount"—boasting the lowest prices in town, bar none.

The Fentons paid a visit to Tony's showroom, happily examined cars. Tony himself came over to try to help them make up their minds.

"I've been watching you," he said with an expansive smile. "I'd like to do something for you. I've got just the car—and you won't believe the price!"

He led them to a gleaming two-tone sedan "loaded with extra equipment."

When he said the Fentons could have it for $2,195, with a $710 down payment, the pair was sold right then and there. They signed a finance application which Tony sent that day to the bank. Three days later they drove their car out of Tony's showroom and began studying the road maps to Florida.

The car was the joy of their lives—until they found a letter in the glove compartment, addressed to a Gerald Thompson at an address in Brooklyn.

"He was probably looking around the showroom and dropped it by mistake," Bill said to Alma. "Might be important. I'll call him."

On the phone Fenton explained: "I just bought this new car and found a letter in the glove compartment addressed to you. Shall I mail it to you?"

After a pause, Thompson said: "Let me get this straight. You're telling me you found a letter of mine in your new car?"

"That's right."

"What's the car look like?"

Bill described it. Then Thompson said: "I'm sorry to have to tell you this, but what you bought is not a new car."

"What do you mean?" stammered Bill.

"That used to be my car," Thompson replied

slowly. "I kept it three months and then sold it because it was a lemon. I put about ten thousand miles on it."

Bill Fenton was close to tears when he appeared that day in the office of former Queens District Attorney Frank O'Connor and told his story. The case was turned over to two Assistant D.A.'s, Francis X. Smith, head of the Rackets Bureau, and Eugene Feldman.

"In your dealings, what convinced you the car was new?" asked Smith.

"Well, to begin with, he *said* it was new," Fenton explained. "They gave me all the papers. The car was a beauty."

"Anything else?"

"Well, no—except that it *smelled* like a new car."

The significance of that remark escaped investigators for the moment. They continued with the inquiry, and established that the car purchased by the Fentons was just one of some forty cars in Queens alone which had recently been given elaborate face liftings. The treatment included turning back the odometer, painting the motor, replacing worn foot pedals and carpeting. As a result, indictments totaling 450 counts were returned by the Grand Jury, with Tony Discount at the head of the list. A letter had brought his downfall.

Only one puzzle remained: the new-car smell.

"That really stumped us for a while," Smith recalled later. "But then one of the members of the ring talked. He described how they had developed a special spray which smelled like a combination of new leather and fresh paint. We got a sample and tried it. If you were blind and someone sprayed a car with this mixture, you would swear it was brand new."

We found that the doctored car racket numbers hundreds of practitioners who operate from coast to coast. Our probe extended from New York to Los Angeles, from Chicago to New Orleans. The annual take in this operation is fantastic.

The official files involving "Georgie Golden Hands" are crammed in bulging folders in the headquarters of the New York City Auto Squad at 400 Broome Street. At this writing, Georgie is doing time. Detective Sergeant Hubert McKenna, the Squad's boss, speaks of him with undisguised respect. "Golden Hands was the best," he says. "He was an artist. He couldn't read or write, but he knew cars—everything about them."

Georgie went to work when he was nine, for a crippled uncle in Brooklyn who was a mechanic. At first, he just ran errands. The uncle, who had learned his trade in Europe, saw a future in the youngster and later taught him the trade: how to pound out fenders and panels, how to weld and how to repair an engine. By the time he was twenty-three, Georgie was as good as they come. The old man died and left him the business.

Georgie prospered. His reputation as an expert "body man" spread. Finally his fame came to the attention of a junkman who was then in the process of organizing a car-theft ring. Golden Hands was just what he needed.

He met with Georgie and explained his gimmick. First, he would steal a late-model car, then buy a second car, an old one. The first would be given a face-lifting by Georgie, while the second would be junked. The papers and the motor numbers from the junked car were to be transferred to the new car, which then would have a brand-new identity.

Georgie agreed to go in with the mob, and it set up headquarters in an old riding academy in the Flushing section of New York. It had six barns and, to keep up appearances, a phony "cowboy" was employed to parade around in a western outfit. Golden Hands was put in charge.

He recruited the best car doctors in the business. Two of them were brothers whose specialty was cutting up cars and welding sections. For the muscle work, he hired an expert sledge man named Johnny, who tipped the scales at 275 pounds. (Johnny had once worked for a garage specializing in insurance cases. His job was to up the damage estimate, which he did with a twenty-pound hammer. He once boasted that every ten minutes of his time meant another $300 for the boss.)

The team worked with several garages which sent them cars for repair. The gang would steal one of the cars, at least as far as official records were concerned, simply by removing the serial-number plate (in most cars this is located on the doorjamb), and switching it with the serial-number plate on a recently-acquired, actually stolen car. This latter auto they would then be ready to sell. The customer who had brought in his car for repairs never knew the difference. He would pay for the repair work and drive off, completely unaware that since the serial-number on his car had been switched, he was now, according to the serial plate, driving a stolen car.

Georgie Golden Hands excelled in removing serial-number plates without leaving a trace. Then he broadened his skills to become an expert in half-breed cars. These were created by taking the least-damaged end of one wrecked car and welding it to the opposite end of another. Thus for a small investment at a junkyard, a nice profit could be made by selling a half-breed as a good used car. Since the two halves are simply welded together, a half-breed collapses like an accordion, of course, if it's in an accident.

"When Georgie got finished, you could never tell," recalls Sergeant McKenna. "Why, he even took cars of different years and joined them. After we rounded up the mob, one of them admitted to stealing over two hundred wrecks which ended up as half-breeds."

Georgie Golden Hands ultimately conducted one of the strangest seminars in the history of the New York City Police Department. He gave a three-hour "lecture" to a group of veteran cops. They sat there like college students, taking notes. Georgie couldn't readily return the handshakes of congratulations when his talk was over —he was in handcuffs.

The city of Newark, New Jersey, was a center for the doctored car gyp until the police moved in. It all started when an irate car owner complained to the then Essex County Prosecutor Charles V. Webb.

"I bought a new car—so I thought—and started

south. It ran exactly one hour and then broke down. I had to get it towed off the highway. That was bad enough. Then, as a mechanic started to look it over, I mentioned that it was brand-new. He turned to me and said, 'Are you crazy? This isn't a new car. It's got a real case of the old-car shakes.' "

The mechanic was right. Prosecutor Webb discovered eventually that the "new car" had served a gruelling stint as a taxicab in Philadelphia and had clocked 60,000 miles.

The prosecutor hit hard. In the resulting investigation, fourteen received jail sentences. Webb, who is now in private law practice in Newark, said recently: "That was a big-business operation. The ring had contacts in at least ten states. They missed nothing, and had the best technicians working for them."

In New York State, Attorney General Louis J. Lefkowitz started a probe, discovered dealers purchasing cars from rental agencies, later offering them as "one-owner" cars.

"Now, there is no car that takes a tougher beating than a rental which is used by many different people," observed Lefkowitz. "They were sold on the basis that they had little mileage. We found most of the cars had done twenty thousand miles or better. But the odometers had been rolled back to eight thousand miles or less. We found, too, that these cars had been driven to and sold in a number of other states."

In New York City, in Washington, D.C., and undoubtedly in other metropolitan areas as well, there are teams of experts who specialize in setting back odometers. Crooked used car dealers call on their talents almost as a matter of course . . . the job can be done in only ten minutes. The situation is serious enough to warrant federal interest: Senator Paul H. Douglas of Illinois plans to introduce a bill making it a federal crime to set back an odometer. (Lefkowitz has already introduced a state measure to the New York Legislature.)

Here are some of the actual case histories uncovered during the Lefkowitz investigation, and what the victims reported:

U.S. Treasury agent: "I feel like an idiot, since my job is tracking down counterfeiters. But a dealer sold me this '61 Ford which he said had had only one owner. The mileage read eight thousand six hundred and seventy. At the price, it looked like a good deal. Then, I found out that the actual mileage was probably over twenty-two thousand." (In this and the following two instances, actual mileage was estimated by experts from the general condition of the car.)

Long Island housewife: "What a line that salesman gave me! I bought the car because I thought I was getting a good deal: the speedometer read only eight thousand two hundred miles. But the police told me the car had probably done more than twenty-eight thousand miles."

U.S. Marine: "I was stationed at Guantanamo Bay and came home on leave. This dealer told me: 'I've got something real good for you, only eight thousand miles.' So I bought it. All cash. I didn't find out he had given me a bum steer until the Attorney General told me the car had done at least twenty-nine thousand miles."

More than a score of similar cases are pending in the courts.

In the doctored car racket, parts are not only purchased from junk yards, rebuilt and sold as new, but generators, starters, carburetors, even engines, are stolen from late model cars and inferior parts substituted. Rarely does the owner discover what has happened. One exception was James Ryan, a stockbroker living in a Westchester suburb who drove into New York City with his wife for an evening at the theater. They pulled into a midtown parking garage; as the attendant made out the ticket, he asked: "How long?"

Ryan told him, "We're going to dinner and then to see *Hello, Dolly!* I guess we'll be back in about four or five hours."

They walked to a nearby restaurant for dinner, but halfway through the meal, Mrs. Ryan began feeling ill. "We'd better turn around and go home," Ryan decided.

Returning to the garage, he explained the situation to the attendant and asked to have his car brought out immediately. The attendant came back five minutes later to advise Ryan: "I'm sorry, but your car is on the second floor in the back. It's all jammed in."

Ryan's demands that something be done merely brought a shrug of the attendant's shoulders. In desperation Ryan went out into the street and spotted a policeman on the corner. He explained the situation, and the officer returned with him to the garage.

"Let's see the car," the patrolman ordered.

Reluctantly the attendant took them upstairs. There, they came upon a most extraordinary scene: the hood of Ryan's car was up, and two mechanics were frantically lowering his engine back into the car with the aid of a block and tackle. Alongside the car was a second motor. It was apparent that the second engine—a rebuilt—was in the process of being substituted for James Ryan's new one.

There can be no official figures, of course, on how many motors are switched in garages and enclosed parking lots. Every new car is a potential target. Explains a veteran mechanic:

"It's a beautiful gimmick. How many car owners would ever know there had been an engine switch? How often does an owner look under the hood? Even if he did, would he notice any difference? Most engines look pretty much alike."

"How difficult is it to make an engine switch?" we asked the mechanic.

"Nothing to it. All that's involved is removing and replacing the engine bolts and the bolts connecting the transmission to the drive shaft. This can be done in an hour and a half with no sweat. The motor is then either sold to a garage customer who is having motor trouble, or it will be peddled to a hot rodder who wants to 'beef up' his car. This constitutes a big market—a very big and growing market."

"What's the profit angle in a switch of engines?" we asked further.

"A 340-hp late model engine will bring $700 without any trouble," he told us.

How can you be on the alert against the doctored car racket?

1. Have an expert estimate actual mileage as against a low-set odometer.

2. Check ownership papers against the serial number to be sure there hasn't been a switch.

3. Check the number on your engine block against the number on your license when picking up your car after you've parked it in an unfamiliar enclosed garage.

4. In addition, follow the guide-lines given in the preceding chapter on used cars.

CHAPTER IV

Cars repairs: the big fix

JOHN GILWORTH, an $80-a-week bank clerk, pulled into a New Jersey service station decorated by a huge, multicolored sign that read, "Automatic Transmissions Overhauled—$49.50!" He told a uniformed service attendant, "I'm having trouble with the transmission. It's not shifting right . . . could you give me some idea what the problem might be?"

"Could be a lot of things," the attendant said. "Leave your car and we'll check it out in the morning. Just give me your phone number."

Gilworth did. And at 11 the next morning he got a telephone call from the shop foreman. "We've run into some problems with your transmission," the foreman began.

"Like what?" Gilworth asked.

"Well, as we were checking it out, it fell apart," the man answered.

Gilworth hesitated a moment, then asked, "What's that going to cost?"

The foreman did some figuring on his end of the phone and came up with a total: "The bill would be $250.10. But of course your car will be like new."

John Gilworth didn't like the deal at all.

"Forget it. That's just too much," he protested. "I'll have a mechanic I know take a look at it."

The foreman came back: "Okay, whatever you say, but there's going to be a charge. It will cost you $70 for us to put the transmission back together again." And he added, "Of course it won't be any better than it was before—and there'll also be a $2.00-a-day storage charge as long as the car is here."

The dispute went on for several days. Gilworth threatened to report the case to the District Attorney's office and the Better Business Bureau, but he agreed, finally, to pay $50, simply because he didn't want to involve himself in a lawsuit which would tie up his car until the matter was settled.

When Gilworth finally took the car to his mechanic friend the vehicle was "road-tested," which was what should have been done to it in the first place. "One of the bands is slipping," the mechanic said after returning to the garage.

"But this joker told me the transmission had fallen apart!"

"Look," the mechanic told his friend Gilworth, "that transmission hasn't even been touched."

The mechanic adjusted the bands. The car worked perfectly. And the bill came to $8.20.

This kind of bilking goes on hundreds of times a day in every part of the U.S. How much does it cost the driving public? A questioning of local, state and federal law enforcement agencies indicates that the tab for the auto repair racket is well in excess of $100,000,000 a year! No one really knows the full story, since most car owners who have been victimized—those who realize it—just don't report their experiences.

Official files bulge with examples of driver ignorance which has been taken advantage of by dishonest auto repair artists:

- A widow's car broke down during a rainy night on the Long Island Expressway. Helpless and frightened, she had her car towed to a garage. "Lady, you need a new motor job," the mechanic said. She ended up with a bill for $250.54. Yet the only trouble had been a blown fuse.

- A teacher left her car in a Los Angeles garage for a check-up. The next day she was handed a bill for $63.40: new generator, spark plugs, points and condenser. A week later she discovered from her husband, returning from a business trip, that he'd had these items replaced just a month before.

- A successful businessman went into a repair shop in Chicago and asked for a carbon-and-valve job. "I want the old carbon taken out and new carbon put in," he explained. "Who said you needed that?" asked the incredulous mechanic. "Some mechanic . . . but I could feel he was going to overcharge me."

  The garage man remained true to his code: Never pass up a sucker! So he did the carbon-and-valve job, consisting of nothing more than a motor clean-up. And the smart businessman got a bill for $58.20.

Our investigation of the auto repair racket began when one of the authors of this book, Sam Crowther, a reporter for *The Journal-American* and a regular contributor to *Argosy,* was assigned by both publications—because both had been receiving complaints from car-owners—to cover the story. We got in touch with the then Queens District Attorney Frank D. O'Connor, now President of New York's City Council, who set up a "task force," consisting of Assistant District Attorney Francis X. Smith, Chief of the Rackets Bureau, and Detective Investigator Gordon O'Neill, to make a complete investigation.

How to start? How to obtain evidence? The old adage, "It takes a thief to catch a thief," was our key.

We knew a mechanic who had recently finished serving a jail term for auto theft—the police had found his garage being used as a hot-car drop. This guy was a pro, and he agreed to help—for a fee, of course.

"There's only one way to expose a gyp in this business," he explained when we all got together. "You've got to set it up. Get a car in perfect condition—then put something out of adjustment. Start checking the service stations and see what they say is wrong. You're gonna be amazed."

We started out with a 1960 Mercury, had it completely checked by a top-flight mechanic—and had him loosen four 9/16-inch bolts on the converter in the automatic transmission. This resulted in a rattle, but otherwise the car ran perfectly. Then we picked a station at random—this one happened to be in Corona, Queens—drove in, and asked for the head mechanic. Out came a man on whose overalls was stitched the name "Moe."

"What seems to be the trouble?" he asked.

"The car is making a funny noise," we told him.

Moe cocked his head, listened to the engine for a few seconds. "Speed it up," he instructed. We did, and the noise disappeared—a point to remember. Moe then shut off the ignition and removed one of the valve covers which is on top of the block on a Mercury. Again he listened.

Suddenly he straightened up, shook his head and announced, "You're in real trouble. One of the rod bearings is gone. You need a complete motor job."

"For just one rod bearing?" we asked innocently.

"That's all you need to ruin the motor," he insisted. "But don't move the car until you get the work done.

Otherwise the whole motor will go. The rod will go right through the engine block."

At this point, a bright-looking young mechanic came over and whispered something to the boss. Moe turned and dismissed him with a sharp, "I'm handling this."

(Some days later, Assistant D.A. Smith brought the young mechanic in for questioning and asked him what he had said to his boss. "I told him I didn't think it was the rod bearing," he answered. "Because when the car was speeded up, the noise stopped. It would have been just the opposite with a rod bearing—the noise would have gotten worse. Moe knew that. But what could I do?")

Back to Moe. "How much will it cost to get the car fixed?" we asked. He moved off to confer with the owner of the station in the office, returned and told us: "We'll give you a complete motor job for a hundred and twenty-five dollars—and it will be guaranteed. You can have the car tomorrow."

We told Moe it was a company car, that we would have to check with the sales manager, and drove off.

But suppose we had ordered the work done. The motor block would probably have been washed down or steam-cleaned to look as if it had been worked on. Yet the car still wouldn't have been "fixed." We might then have been told something like: "The trouble in the engine 'opened up' the transmission seals." If we'd seemed sufficiently ignorant, we'd probably have been stuck for an additional $200 to $300.

We discovered in the course of our investigation that many of the gyp mechanics have their own personalized gimmicks in trapping the sucker. No matter what's wrong with your car, the bogus repairman's own "specialty" is sure to be involved. There are mechanics who push batteries, some who unload fuel pumps, others who favor generators, voltage regulators, or starters. In the trade, these are known as "parts pushers." They aren't mechanics; they don't know how to fix anything. It's always, "You need a new one."

One character was big on defective carburetors. Our informants took a 1961 Olds to him for a check because of trouble starting. Immediately it was, "You need a new carburetor." Our friend wanted to know why. "It's got rotten parts," was the fantastic answer.

We met another prize operator named Dan who, we were told, was undisputed king of the muffler pushers. To make our test car sound sick this time, an expert police mechanic crossed two wires leading from the plugs to the distributor, causing the motor to miss. That was all we did. There was *nothing* wrong with the muffler.

When we pulled into Dan's station, he was, of course, changing a muffler. He came out from under the rack and inquired, "What seems to be the matter?"

"The car doesn't sound right," we told him. He stalked around the auto like a lion moving in for the kill. He skipped the usual routine of raising the hood and examining the motor. Dan plays it by ear.

"Hmmm," he murmured.

"What's the matter?"

"Your muffler's broke," he announced.

"How did that happen?" Detective O'Neill asked.

"It shook loose and caved in."

"How much for a new one?"

"That'll be eighteen dollars—and the muffler is guaranteed to last the life of the car," he said. We didn't bite.

We later learned more about Dan from some of his victims. One motorist, who really needed a muffler, came to Dan's, parked his car, went into the shop, and started talking to the manager.

Suddenly a mechanic popped his head in the door: "Who owns that Plymouth?"

The motorist admitted that he did.

The mechanic took him outside and began to rock the car back and forth. "Look," he said, "your shocks are shot. They're resting on the springs."

The Plymouth owner agreed to a new set of shocks for $31.97, plus a new muffler with a tailpipe. When he picked up his car the next day, the total tab was $51.97.

Ten days later the man began having muffler trouble with the Plymouth. Indignantly he returned to Dan's, parked in the same place and went into the office to complain. As he was waiting to see the manager, still another mechanic rushed in to ask, "You own that Plymouth out there?"

"Yes," he said suspiciously, "why?"

"Your shocks are shot!"

This shock-absorber racket is widespread. There have been many instances where absolutely nothing was wrong with the shocks—customers got nothing more than a coat of quick-drying paint to make old shock absorbers appear new.

Then there was Freddie, whose claim to fame, in our books, rests on his contribution to the terminology of the auto-repair racket. When we pulled into his garage in Long Island City, the "trouble" again was that "the car doesn't sound right."

Freddie didn't waste any time. He yanked open the hood, took a fast look and declared seriously: "Your car's been hit by the white flash."

There was a moment of dumbfounded silence. Then Detective O'Neill asked, "It got hit by *what?*"

"Haven't you heard of the white flash?" he asked with a straight face. "It's like a bolt of lightning. It's rare—but when you get the flash everything goes. The whole motor has to be re-wired." He calculated an estimate of the damage—$33.10.

(He made no offer to check on whether the fuse might have burned out. This would have been the first thing an honest mechanic did.)

At this point, we asked: "If everything has been burned out, how were we able to get to your station?"

It didn't phase him. "Just luck," he said readily.

In days gone by, the car owner rarely changed spark plugs. Once in a while, you would have them out, cleaned and, perhaps, re-gapped. Today, the gyp mechanic will try to sell you a set of new plugs every chance he gets.

To smoke out a crooked operator we'd heard about in Jamaica, Long Island ("Louis would push new plugs if you drove in with a flat tire") we switched distributor wires. Driving into Louis' service station in Jamaica, we complained that the car "didn't have any pep."

He lifted the hood, listened, then instructed us to shut off the motor.

(Note that Louis did not follow the customary procedure of "shorting out" each plug to discover which one wasn't firing.)

Then, with a socket wrench, he removed a brand-new plug. "Just as I thought," he announced. "Your plugs collapsed."

"They what?"

"They bent over . . . I'll show you."

If you're not looking closely, Louis' hand is quicker than your eye. But we watched closely enough to see him give the outside electrode a deft tap. The action naturally rendered the plug useless.

"Look," he instructed us, pointing to the electrodes, "there's supposed to be a space there for the spark to jump. But now it shorts out." Of course.

We wanted to know if he had many cases like this. "Oh yes," he said. "It happens with late model cars. There's too much compression and it bends the points."

"How about the other plugs?" we asked.

"They're gone too," he announced. "When one goes, they all go."

(No expert with whom we checked had ever heard of all eight plugs "collapsing" at the same time.)

Other gyp mechanics, we learned, "collapse" plugs by "accidentally" knocking the electrode against the engine block as the plug is removed. In any case, it's a profitable racket. First, the mechanic sells, for ten dollars or more, a set which is unnecessary. Then he cleans up the old plugs—which are generally not really old—and sells them as new ones to a second sucker.

Batteries represent the biggest single replacement item in cars. Battery thieves are in debt to the world of electronics, which produced the electric battery tester. In the hands of an honest service man, this is a most accurate device. But with a little finagling, you can make a tester show anything you want it to.

For this phase of our investigation, we took a new battery, dirtied it with grease and grime, and ran it down. There was nothing wrong; all the battery needed was a charge.

We drove into a service station in Long Island City and complained: "We have trouble getting started."

The station, we knew, was the headquarters of a battery specialist. His interest was immediately obvious—the shop was littered with batteries of all shapes and sizes.

Sure enough, the man, whose name was Benny, made a predictable first move: he picked up a battery tester and lifted the hood of our car. He took the two electrodes and applied them to cell number one. The indicator swung to "good" in the green zone of the tester.

"This cell is okay," he said.

He shifted to cell number two—but this time he switched the two electrodes, causing the battery to "short-out." The pointer started to flutter and ended up at the sick end of the dial.

"There's your trouble," said Benny. "A bum cell. The battery's no good."

Then he made his pitch. A new battery would be

$28, with five off for the old one. If we'd fallen for his deal, our battery would have been "rebuilt," and then sold by Benny as new.

Pete was another champ on our list of crooked mechanics. Like the others he had his specialty: points. This is a switch-like device, located in the distributor, which regulates the flow of current to the spark plugs. We tested Pete at a service station in Fresh Meadows.

He pulled up the hood and zeroed in on the distributor like a hawk after a rabbit. In nothing flat he had the distributor cap off and out came the points. Exhibiting them in the palm of his hand, he announced: "There's your trouble. The points are burned out."

"How can you tell?" we wanted to know.

"See for yourself—they're black."

Well, the points in the Mercury we were using *were* black. It's a special coating put on to prevent corrosion, except on the firing surfaces. But we weren't, of course, supposed to know that.

Unfortunately, the American car owner doesn't have much of a chance against gyp mechanics. These characters have *legal* protection. It's what is known as the Mechanic's Lien. This exists in many parts of the country, and what it boils down to is that once you place your car in the hands of a garageman, you are at the service man's complete mercy. *You can be billed for any amount he decides on.* Even a murderer has the right of *habeas corpus*—but an auto serviceman *can hold your car until you pay.* A car owner going into civil court is usually wasting his time. It's your word against the mechanic's—he qualifies as an expert, and you don't.

Some of the swindles perpetrated on unsuspecting car owners are almost incredible. One in the roster of gyps was a mechanic who would approach a car owner and declare: "Your car has no market value because it's too old. But that steering wheel is an *antique,* and dealers are crazy for them. So if you buy a car from me, I'll put your steering wheel in it. Then, if you want you can turn around and sell the car at a nice profit."

It's hard to believe anyone would fall for such a line, but official records show that they have. This is what crooks trade on—the sheer gullibility of the public.

Not long ago, one of us took his car to a neighborhood garage for a slow charge—the battery had run down as a result of the car's not having been used for a number of weeks.

When he returned next day, the service man said: "Your car is hard to start. You need a lot of work: new plugs, new points, a tune-up, and probably a new generator."

There was, however, one slight detail of which the service man was unaware. A few months before, the keys had been lost. And since then, the car had had to be started by "jumping" the ignition system.

The service man was told: "Get in the car and start it."

He did, and began fumbling around the dashboard. "Where's the key?" he asked.

"There isn't any key," he was told. "Now how come

you said the car was hard to start when obviously you didn't even try?"

He tried to laugh it off. "If you don't like it, sue me."

His attitude was typical. How can the average car owner protect himself? Here are ten tips from the American Automobile Association:

1. Get to know your car. Study the owner's manual. It contains a wealth of information and has been prepared by the person who knows your car best—the manufacturer. This won't make you an expert, but at least you won't be completely in the dark.
2. Know your service man. If possible, avoid doing business with a stranger. Pick out an authorized, franchised dealer, or a competent neighborhood mechanic who looks upon you as a potential long-term customer. A garage which supplies you with gas and oil on a regular basis is more likely to give you a fair shake than some highway service station operator who never expects to see you again.
3. Be as specific as possible in saying what you feel is wrong. Don't make such statements as "The car doesn't sound right . . . will you check it?" This is an open invitation to a gyp artist.
4. Don't leave your car in a garage and say you'll be back later. Stick around and watch while

the mechanic checks your car. You may not know what's going on . . . but the repairman may *think* you do, and he'll be less inclined to treat you as a sucker.

5. Beware of any repairman who, after a one-minute check of your car, comes up with some diagnosis like "your motor is burned up" or "the shocks are falling out."
6. If you are told that major repair is involved but that the car is driveable, shop around and see what other garages have to say. With two or three estimates to choose from, the odds of getting stuck are lessened.
7. When repairs are definitely involved, get an estimate *in writing* on the garage's letterhead. The estimate should specify both parts and labor. When a new or rebuilt unit is required, ask for a guarantee and have *it* in writing, too.
8. If you agree to have a new part installed, ask to see it in its original container. This is especially important in the case of spark plugs, points, starters, generators, fuel pumps.
9. If you are buying a rebuilt part, ask to see the tag attached by the rebuilder, or the box in which it is returned. This will help prevent your getting stuck with a unit which has just been given a fast once over.
10. When a price for repairs is quoted, ask how this compares with what is known as the "manual" price. There are several "bibles" in the

trade which list accepted charges for various types of work. If you are quoted a price much over this, walk out.

One bright glow in an otherwise dark picture is cast by the new car "analysts" who sell nothing, make no repairs, are not an extension of any manufacturer, but exist only, as *Time* magazine recently stated, "to examine an automobile from its exhaust pipe to its headlights and report just what is wrong with it and what is not." At one such analyst in Denver, for instance, your car is given an impartial, hour-long series of some 100 tests in an 80-foot-long laboratory containing 77 various pieces of equipment. The fee is $20.00. "In most instances," *Time* declares, "the company's findings simply point up the shoddy if not shady job many garages do." Ford's E. B. Rickard calls the service, "Just like modern medicine." It may be a remedy for some of the evils.

But what about a long-range legislative program to beat the repair gyps? Here are two measures which have been presented recently to the New York State Legislature:

- License all mechanics; give rigid examinations, require minimum standards of experience, such as required by the FAA for airplane mechanics. This has received strong support from some independent owners as well as unions—such as Local 3 of the United Auto Workers. (Unions are against gas-pumpers doing business as "mechanics.")

- Set up a system whereby car owners would have legal recourse in cases where they feel they have been victimized. This should be done by a board of experts competent to judge the evidence—a board whose roster might include an attorney, a master mechanic, and representatives of garage labor and management organizations. This would be a start. It is high time the American car owner was granted his own Bill of Rights.

CHAPTER V

Tired to death

POLICE PATROLS on super highways throughout the country are in complete accord about one of their single biggest headaches: faulty tires. On U.S. high-speed highways, tire failure is two to three times greater than it is on local stop-and-go roads. Bill Davidson, director of information for the New York State Thruway, reports: "In 1964 there were a total of 17,416 cases in which our emergency service trucks responded to motorists who had tire trouble. These were only *officially recorded* cases. There is no count of the cases in which motorists changed tires without requesting assistance. I would say conservatively that the total number would triple the number we know about."

Davidson tells of his own first-hand experience: "Driving on the Thruway, I've seen tires disintegrate right before my eyes. Once as I was leaving Rochester, a truck five or six lengths ahead of me suddenly blew a tire—and it spattered my windshield with particles of rubber. I pulled off the road to have a look. Pieces of rubber were not only all over my car but extended down the highway.

"Collecting rubber which has been torn from tires," Davidson goes on, "has become a major maintenance problem on the Thruway. Every day our trucks gather up bushel-baskets of rubber—all from tires which have gone to pieces under turnpike stress."

Senator Gaylord Nelson of Wisconsin recently testified that tires were to blame for 7 per cent of all highway fatalities.

On the Kansas Turnpike not long ago, a sedan shot past a patrol car at an estimated 85 mph. As the highway patrolman started to radio ahead for a road block, he heard a loud explosion, followed by the sickening sounds of a crash. He rushed to the scene to find that the sedan had rolled over what later proved to be nine times, killing all three occupants. Investigation showed that the driver had been speeding on recapped snow tires which had blown. The top safe speed for recapped snow tires, according to experts, is about 40 mph.

It's a good idea for the motorist to understand some of the elementary aspects of physics as they relate to tires. When you brake at a speed of 50 mph, a centrifugal force of two tons is trying to tear your tires apart. Slamming on your brakes at 35 mph will tear off an amount of rubber which under ordinary driving conditions would carry your car one road mile. Three hard brakings at 60 mph in rapid succession can generate 500 degrees of heat —and rubber begins the disintegration process at temperatures above 250 degrees.

In Nevada not long ago, A. H. Fuller, president of the Fuller Brush Company, and his wife died when a tire blew at an estimated 125 mph. Fuller, a long-time sports car enthusiast, was driving his imported racer, which was capable of doing 145 mph. Though not pushing the car over its limit, what he didn't know was that the tires, original equipment, were not made to handle the speed the car was capable of doing. The tires had been designed for ordinary driving.

This case illustrates a point which speed-loving teenagers and adults would do well to keep in mind: Many cars sold today are equipped with tires which are not capable of standing up under speeds which the car can achieve.

Automobile tires are at present the subject of intensive government investigation. Testifying before the Federal Trade Commission in 1965, Harry C. McCreary, Jr., chairman of the McCreary Tire and Rubber Company of Indiana, Pennsylvania, dealt several raps to the automobile industry. He declared that regulations should be put into effect to make it unlawful for tire companies to sell tires "which are not large enough to support the load imposed when a car is carrying its full load of passengers and up to 200 pounds of luggage in the trunk."

McCreary indicated that the tire industry has tried for years, through the Tire and Rim Association, to establish maximum tire carrying-capacity weights. "But these efforts have been largely ignored by Detroit engineers. They insist on equipping their new cars with tires designed to carry the empty vehicles, plus two-and-a-half passengers."

One of the quickest ways to ruin a perfectly good tire, McCreary told the Commission, is to pile onto it a greater load than it is designed to carry. Most tires can safely carry a 20 per cent overload, provided the inflation pressure is kept up to 24 pounds minimum. But McCreary said this point is ignored. "Let the overload rise to 50 per cent, let the inflation pressure drop off to 20 pounds or so, and the occupants of that particular car are in a very dangerous situation."

McCreary told the probers that the automobile companies are "Very Important Customers" in Akron. When Detroit snaps its fingers Akron jumps through hoops—backwards if necessary. "For many years," he stressed, "Detroit had made the decisions as to what kind of tires should be put on the average automobile."

In advance of the public hearings it held (in January 1965), the FTC expressed what could have been the understatement of the year: "Consumers are often confused and deceived in buying replacement tires for their automobiles."

The FTC found extensive use made of advertising which purports to offer tires at substantial savings or reductions in price. The so-called "list" or "no-trade-in" price is, for the most part, a fiction. This is generally not the price at which tires are sold because in most instances the purchaser has a used tired to trade in. To complicate matters further, tires are normally sold at substantial discounts from the so-called "list" price, with or without a trade-in.

The subject of tire "guarantees" also came under attack by the FTC. Guarantees, the Commission learned, offer nothing the purchaser would not receive *without* a guarantee: the mumbo-jumbo is meaningless. The guarantee relates to a "list" price which is fictitious. Most guarantees provide for a credit "in proportion to the guarantee time, or the tread remaining at the time of adjustment."

A case history from FTC files will illustrate: "I bought a tire for $16 which was guaranteed for 24 months. I was told at the time that the tire had a list price of $24. The tire failed after sixteen months. I went back to the dealer and was told that I was entitled to a credit of one-third, or $8 toward the purchase of a tire at the 'list' or 'no-trade-in price' of $24. Under the guarantee, I ended up paying $16 for the new tire, which is the same price I'd have paid without the guarantee."

This is just part of the story. Talking of the questionable marketing practices used by manufacturers, dealers, and garages, a spokesman for the FTC told us: "Tires are usually advertised in a way that gives the buyer no clear information about the grade or quality of the tire being advertised. Whether a tire is second, third, or fourth grade is generally not disclosed in the ad. Similar brand names are frequently used for different grades, or lines, of tires. For example, adjectives like 'super' and 'deluxe' appear not only in the brand names of 'premium' tires, but in first, second, and third line tires as well. The only clue usually furnished as to tire grade is price. When the tire is offered at a purported bargain, price may serve to mislead rather than enlighten as to the grade or line of the tire advertised."

The total absence of any recognized system for grade labeling or quality rating of tires serves to compound the confusion. There simply is no basis for a comparison of various tire brands.

On this subject, testimony before the FTC consisted mostly of double talk. When called upon, industry representatives only added to general bewilderment. Here is the actual testimony of John F. Floberg, Secretary and General Counsel of the Firestone Tire and Rubber Company:

"The factors which determine quality and grade of the tire are many and are subject to differences of opinions and in some cases are subjective. Every tire, like most products, represents an accommodation between conflicting considerations and, except for the fact that safety is never compromised by Firestone, stressing one desirable quality of tire can easily force reduction of emphasis on a different desirable quality. There seems to be some notion prevalent that the quality of a tire can be authoritatively adjudicated by some simply objective tests which would include measurements of weight, physical dimensions, numbers of plies, thickness of tread and perhaps a couple of other simple external features. This concept is as fallacious, however, as would be determining the quality of a book by its size, weight, and number of pages. Whether an item be a diamond or an airplane or a painting or virtually any other consumer item, physical dimensions and quality are quite distinguishable considerations. The same is true of tires."

To put it simply—something Mr. Floberg is unable to do—he is against any system for grading tires. In sympathy with Floberg was Herbert G. Smith, Vice-President of U.S. Rubber. Mr. Smith declared that grading would require "extremely complicated engineering, chemical, and process specifications which probably would not be capable of application by all industry members."

Then he added, "Such specifications would certainly act as a brake on continued improvement of safety and endurance features—areas in which the industry has been outstanding over the past years."

Underlying these protests there is a real, if unconfessed, reason for the tire companies' reluctance to have tire quality clearly graded. It is simply that big manufacturers do not make tires only for sale under their own names. They also make cheaper, un-named "lines" which they sell to a variety of retail outlets—which then market the tires under *their* names. In marketing, these outlets are at liberty to invent their own grades, coin their own descriptive adjectives, and adjust their own prices. It would hardly do the manufacturers' supply business any good to have uniform grading enforced. It would, in fact, benefit no one but the consumer to know what he was getting for his money.

What the consumer should know, principally, is how much rubber a tire has on it. The more rubber there is, the safer the tire and the more it will cost—and so, generally speaking, the more a tire costs, the better it is. When professional self-interest is involved, safety is the first consideration; taxicab fleet owners and trucking operators, for instance, put out huge sums to get the best tires they can.

John Floberg of Firestone offered this defense to the FTC on the subject of tire safety, "Of all the millions of tires manufactured annually by Firestone, there have not, in any one year since I have been working for Firestone, been as many as ten lawsuits—and usually the number has been smaller—filed against the company involving automobile accidents which might plausibly be attributed to failures of these tires."

Then the New York Automobile Association made its appearance before the Committee and the FTC heard a spokesman describe how the AAA, in 1962, had called for the adoption of safety performance standards for new tires. "We knew from past experience that safety equipment is not put on new cars, unless such items are mandated by law or at least until there is a threat of such action."

Senator Edward J. Speno, former chairman of the New York State Legislative Committee on Motor Vehicles and Traffic Safety, joined the AAA in what has developed into a long, uphill battle to assure motorists of safer tires. Again, the fundamental tire problem was the confusion over the multiplicity of descriptions given to tires—meaningless designations and phrases deliberately designed to bewilder the buying public.

"With the price of tires ranging from $7.50 to $100, price was of limited help in making a determination of quality and durability," the AAA charged. "We interviewed dealers who admitted their shelves were stocked with tires they would not advise drivers to use on high-speed turnpikes. Obviously, if this question was not raised by the purchaser, he would be totally unaware of the danger to his own life and the life of others on the highway."

Maurice Gladman, President of the National Tire Dealers and Retreaders Association, warned that "the advertising of phony bargains should be halted by the FTC, which should put new teeth into its rules against deceptive pricing." Gladman advised the Commission that "abandoning outdated and outmoded terminology in advertising would aid public understanding." He said "such terms as ply-rating have no uniform meaning." He charged that it meant one thing to one company and a completely different thing to another.

Then came the question: Are manufacturers' list prices fictitious or merely confusing? Edwin H. Sonnecken, director of Goodyear's corporate planning and research, added to the double talk on the term "no-trade-in" price. He testified that this represents a "bench mark" or, he said, "the offering price."

"But how many sales are made at this price?" one Commission member asked.

"There might be many sales at that price," was the evasive answer.

This shook up Commissioner Philip Elman, who interrupted to ask: "You mean you're supposed to haggle? Do you mean I've been missing out on something?"

If the experts are confused, what about the rest of us?

Maurice Gladman, of the Tire Dealers and Retreaders Association, expressed the hope that the FTC hearings would stimulate voluntary and corrective action within the industry—and hoped that government intervention would come only when all voluntary measures had been exhausted. Meanwhile, death continues to ride the highways.

The most death-dealing of all tire practices is that of regrooving. This is done with a special machine which makes the tire look new. Although there is practically no rubber left, the tire is sold as a "factory outlet"—another meaningless merchandising term that just means "cheap tire."

"This practice is criminal," says an investigator in New Orleans. "A motorist traveling at turnpike speeds on a set of regrooved tires is a prime candidate for the cemetery, and will probably take a few people with him."

A woman in Oregon reported: "I bought four tires, on sale, which I was told were new. A week later I had a flat. I told the garageman, 'This flat must be a freak. I just got these tires—all new.'

" 'Lady,' the garageman said, 'those are old tires that have been regrooved. You were lucky you didn't have something worse than a leak. You could have been killed!' "

In many instances of tire trouble, the motorist is to blame because he fails to replace tires when he should. A few years back, an investigation was launched on the Pennsylvania Turnpike after a series of accidents during the months of July and August. It was discovered that sixty-eight of the accidents involving skids were the fault of tires.

Skids in the summer months? Didn't make sense. At first, the police wrote off the accidents as "too fast for conditions." Then further investigation revealed that in certain areas, flash thundershowers were common. As a result, unseen oil slicks, floating on the rain water, were a "hidden hazard in the case of bald tires." Here is some of the testimony that was uncovered:

- A motorist whose death was the result of a "junk tire" was found wearing a $35 pair of shoes and a new Stetson. But apparently he had decided he didn't have enough money for new tires.

- DOA, the police blotter read. The daughter of a wealthy Philadelphia family and her two school friends, all killed when their car skidded into a tractor-trailer. Investigators found the left rear tire worn down to what is known as the "breaker strip," a strip of rubber applied in the course of manufacture which is about the last thing to go before the actual cord fabric.

- A secretary spent $350 on a set of golf clubs—but was killed on the way to a golf course when a bald tire blew out and her car hit a tree.

These are all examples of foolhardy economy—car owners trying to squeeze the last dime's worth of mileage out of their well-worn tires. It is a death-defying attitude.

The Pennsylvania State Police, determined to do something about shoddy tires, enlisted the help of toll collectors stationed at the entrances to the Turnpike. In addition, they checked tires of cars parked in gasoline service centers. Some 3,644 warnings were issued for unsafe tires; 500 drivers were ordered off the pike because of the poor condition of their tires; another 610 had to replace a tire regarded as weak with a spare before being permitted to proceed. The result? A sharp drop in summer skidding accidents. After the first reports came in, other toll roads instituted similar systems.

Thanks to 1964 legislation, New York state and local police now have the authority to stop motorists and make an examination of the depth of the tread—1/16th of an inch of rubber, measurable with a special gauge, is the minimum allowed. The same bill made it illegal to sell regrooved tires in New York. (Colorado and California are two other states in which it is illegal; Massachusetts, Michigan and Pennsylvania have legislation pending.)

What can the motorist do to protect himself in the buying and care of tires? Here are ten suggestions:

1. Watch out for bargains on either new or recapped tires. If you know the outlet to be a reliable one, you *may* get a good buy.

2. Make certain you buy the right sized tire for your car; consult the auto manufacturer's owner manual for a mention of the proper size.

3. If you do any turnpike driving, spend a little extra money for heavy-duty tires. They are safer and will last longer.

4. Make a point of having your tire pressure checked regularly—few car owners remember to do this. Check your owner's manual. If you do much high speed driving, add four to six pounds. *Ignore* the advice that's often given: "For long distance driving, bleed your tires." Studies have shown that under-inflation can weaken a tire more quickly than any other factor.

5. From time to time make a visual check. You don't have to be an expert to detect a crack in the casing.

6. Check wheel alignment. Trouble here can cut the life of your tires by as much as 50 per cent. The symptom: excessive wear on one side of the tire. (This kind of wear can also mean your wheels are out of balance, so check *that,* too.)

7. Look for excessive wear around both the outer edges of a tire. It's a danger signal of *under-inflation.*

8. Try not to climb or hit the curb when parking—particularly if you own tubeless tires. This is even more dangerous if you have sub-standard tires.

9. If you have a blow-out, take your foot off the gas at once. Don't apply the brakes until the car has lost most of its speed. Otherwise, you may lose control and jump into an on-coming lane.

Good tires are probably the cheapest life insurance a car owner can buy. Whether you live or die on a highway may depend on a ball of cord from a textile factory, a pail of compound from a synthetic rubber factory, and a few pounds of air from a compressor in a service station. For the sake of your life, buy the best tires and check them regularly.

CHAPTER VI

No money down—but plenty to pay

THE OLD BLUE BOMB was using too much oil. It had lasted through 110,000 rugged miles and now required more service than it was worth. Eddie Phillips, who lived outside Chicago and drove an hour from home to office and back again each day, had about decided it was time to put the old car out to pasture.

One day, on the return trip from work, Eddie succumbed to the lure of a car lot that advertised: "Easy Payments Arranged!" The thing was on his mind. This seemed the time to make a move, and he drove in. The showroom offered half a dozen new cars but the really "great buys," according to a prominent sign, were among the sixty used cars in the lot. Each had been polished to a high shine and decorated with a bargain price tag.

Eddie had no sooner shut off his motor than a salesman stepped over, glanced at the old blue car and pronounced judgment brightly, "I'd say that heap has just about had it."

Eddie couldn't help but nod in agreement, as the salesman went on: "Don't worry, you've come to the right place—some beauties have just been moved into the lot. And we've got a new special plan. You can drive the car right off the lot . . . *with no down payment.*"

The pitch was smooth and Eddie Phillips needed a "no down payment" deal. The salesman showed him several "beauties" and Eddie liked a sedan at $1,595 best. The car was a "steal," according to the salesman, who added *sotto voce* that it had undoubtedly been mispriced.

"What will you allow me for my car?" Eddie asked, all caution tossed to the winds.

The salesman, who had already implied that Eddie's car was ready for the scrap heap, now took a second deliberately long look. "I tell you what I'm going to get the boss to agree to," he said finally, "a two-hundred dollar allowance."

He waited just long enough for the impact of his generosity to sink in, then added, "And remember what else: no down payment. The car is yours for thirty-five bucks a month!"

Eddie went eagerly into the office and signed some papers. There was a good deal of fine print, but he didn't bother reading it. Within minutes, he was driving his new used car off the lot.

A couple of months later, Eddie got a $10 raise and decided to increase his payment on the car to $50 a month. He called the car dealer and was turned over to the bookkeeper. He explained to the girl that he wanted to raise his monthly payments.

"I'm sorry, but you can't do that," he was astonished to hear. "You are bound by the original agreement to pay thirty-five dollars a month."

Then he asked what turned out to be a very good, but slightly overdue, question. "When I finish paying for this car, how much will it have cost me?"

The bookkeeper shuffled through the records and rather reluctantly gave him the answer: $3,145.20.

If a chagrined Eddie Phillips had not gone to the authorities with details of this transaction he would have had to pay over $1,500 in interest for a $1,595 purchase. He brought the case to the Chicago Better Business Bureau, which pressured the dealer into working out a settlement.

This case is typical enough. Automobile financing is one of the most lucrative rackets in America today.

Senator Paul H. Douglas of Illinois, chairman of a Banking and Currency Committee's Subcommittee, has conducted extensive hearings on the car-finance racket. He told us:

"The American car owner pays $2,000,000,000 a year more than he should in the buying of new and used cars. The practice of misrepresenting the true cost of financing cars is widespread. Many car owners don't realize how they are gypped by unscrupulous dealers who talk them into contracts which never give the true picture of what they are ultimately going to pay. They are caught up in a miasma of double talk, fine print and false representation from which, in most cases, they have no recourse."

Asked about the complications of auto finance contracts, he said: "In many states they are so complicated that most *lawyers* don't understand them. There's too much mumbo-jumbo."

"Is the individual car salesman part of the conspiracy?" we asked.

"Not necessarily," Senator Douglas replied. "He's given a lot of charts that tell him what to charge, but he doesn't always really know what he is charging for. I wouldn't blame it all on the salesman. In many cases, he is being taken in as much as the unsuspecting fellow buying the car."

During the extensive hearings (from 1960 through 1963) of Senator Douglas' Subcommittee, John J. O'Brien took the witness stand in the big paneled hearing room and identified himself as president and general manager of the Better Business Bureau of Greater St. Louis. He said:

"I am here to discuss with you the background of what is known as the 'pack,' which is used extensively in some automobile time contracts. [The 'pack' referred to is the insertion of extras charged in a finance contract. It applies not only to automobiles but to other retail contracts for commodities where financing is involved.] The public is unconscionably gouged of millions of dollars each year at the hands of some auto dealers—sometimes with the active encouragement of certain finance companies.

"Please understand," he added, "that this is by no means an attack upon the automobile industry nor upon automobile dealers and financial institutions of good repute who have, through the complex economy of time payment financing, placed America on wheels and enabled our people to enjoy the pleasures and conveniences of mass transportation on a mutually satisfactory pay-as-you-go basis."

After paying this tribute, O'Brien went on to some damning revelations.

He testified: "A multiplicity of [interest] rate charts is provided to the dealer so he can simply select the one best suited to his needs, or the gullibility of his customer. In such cases, by prearrangement with certain unscrupulous auto dealers and a few unscrupulous finance companies, the 'pack' is set up. Persons with poor credit are also supposed to pay a higher rate. Some charts include insurance coverage, some do not. Seldom can the purchaser tell what he is getting. Unhappily this system goes on in many states where no control is exerted over time-finance contracts of this type."

Senator Douglas cut in: "Just a minute, Mr. O'Brien. This is a very serious charge. Do you mean to say that the finance company gives the dealer a hunting license to get as high finance charges as he can from the individual buyer?"

O'BRIEN: "I do."

DOUGLAS: "This is based on a wide study on your part?"

O'BRIEN: "Yes, sir. And I have affidavits to prove it."

O'Brien then introduced into evidence three rate charts—all showing the amount which the finance company agrees to kick back to the dealer.

DOUGLAS: (holding up the three charts) "Do you mean on this first interest rate chart, the dealer gets $96?"

O'BRIEN: "Right."

DOUGLAS: "On the second chart, he get $150?"

O'BRIEN: "Right."

DOUGLAS: "On the third chart, he gets $163?"

O'BRIEN: "Exactly."

Mr. O'Brien went on to discuss what is known in the trade as the "balloon note." This is a note that has been refinanced. If a car buyer cannot afford monthly payments large enough to purchase the car over an allowed two or three year payment program, an agreement is worked out for him to make smaller monthly payments; at the end of the period he is to pay off the balance in one lump sum. As he is not likely to be able to make this final payment, he will, at the time it is due, refinance the note, possibly with another balloon note.

O'Brien cited the case of a man in Cleveland who

had bought a car for $2,543.64, with the understanding that he would make a final payment of $1,993. When the time came, he didn't have the $1,993, and had to refinance. By the time he had finally discharged his debt on the car, he'd paid a total of 49 per cent interest.

An even more startling case was one Mr. O'Brien cited as having happened in Baton Rouge. A car there was bought on a balloon note for $1,730. It had to be refinanced several times. Before the owner was through, he wound up paying 410 per cent in interest!

The car owner, seeking the easy road to soft credit, has made himself the prime target of the nation's moneylenders.

Extraordinary testimony on consumer finance was also given by William McChesney Martin, Chairman of the Board of Governors of the Federal Reserve System:

SENATOR DOUGLAS: "What do you think is the general thesis on how the rate of interest should be expressed?"

MR. MARTIN: "I will have to be honest with you. It has been confusing to me, on a number of occasions on transactions that I have been involved in, to try to figure out just exactly what it is."

SENATOR DOUGLAS: "You mean the present practices are confusing?"

MR. MARTIN: "Not only the present practices are confusing, but how you figure it is confusing. Take an automobile that has fire insurance, burglary insurance, and theft insurance, and other things on it. You trade in an old car, and you try to figure the unpaid balance. The purchaser may be willing to pay for the car *in toto,* you see, but he wants to know what it would cost him if he financed the balance, including the cost of insurance and other charges involved in the use of credit."

SENATOR DOUGLAS: "If this is confusing to you, who was president of the New York Stock Exchange and Assistant Secretary of the Treasury, what do you suppose it is to the man working for wages? Let me ask you this question: Suppose a man buys, on the installment plan, an automobile at $2,500, with $500 down, and the original unpaid balance is $2,000, therefore. He is told that the rate of interest on this is 6 per cent and 6 per cent is computed on the $2,000 of the unpaid balance. It comes to $120 per year, or $300 for 2½ years, and he is given, let us say, 30 months in which to pay this. He pays it off at the rate of $66.67 a month, plus an interest charge of $10 a month.

"In the first month, that is 6 per cent, but with a declining balance he is paying $10 on that last installment at the end of the 30 months of $66.67, is he not? And that comes to, on a yearly rate, $120 on $66.67, or roughly 180 per cent interest.

"Do you think the interest should be charged as a percentage of the original obligation or as a percentage of the outstanding unpaid obligation?"

MR. MARTIN: "I think it should be charged as a percentage of the outstanding unpaid obligation. That is the logical thing."

Some of the best testimony during the hearings came from Hillel Black, a free lance writer and reporter who had described his experiences in a book called *Buy Now, Pay Later*. Black told Senator Douglas and Senator Bennett:

"A new entrepreneur has entered the American marketplace. Actually we have known him for a long time. In fact, we have been dealing with him ever since we purchased our first car or refrigerator or, for that matter, hairpins or girdles. This new entrepreneur is our local auto dealer, department store owner, or Main Street retailer. We once knew him as a seller of merchandise. What perhaps many of us do not know is that merchandise in many instances no longer is his main item. The new item that he now wants to sell us is debt."

SENATOR BENNETT: "In a prior statement, you say: 'The irony is that in his own country, the American consumer who buys on time is treated like an ignorant tourist in a foreign land. Incapable of even translating the value of the coin he uses, he readily accepts the first price given him.' I congratulate you on your ability to put words together, but what does it mean?"

MR. BLACK: "Sir, what I am trying to say is that it sort of works two ways. On one hand, the American consumer cannot figure out what he is paying when he pays on time, and he just goes and buys. And on the other hand, he is not told.

"Another point that should be made here, too, is that when people buy on time, what they frequently will ask is: What is it going to cost me a month? In many instances, they do not bother to add it all up and find out what the total cost would be. This monthly charge sometimes adds up to more than the buyer can afford."

There are plenty of case histories to illustrate the fact that dealers don't want to sell for cash. The money is made in financing.

One of New York City's best known news photographers, a friend of ours, walked into an automobile showroom recently and told the salesman he wanted a four-door sedan, indicating a specific make and color.

"I'll pay cash."

The salesman stared at him as if he had just ordered a space ship. "Why? Nobody does."

"I have the money," the photographer said. "Why should I be annoyed with monthly payments?"

The salesman insisted: "You're much better off financing."

"Look," the photographer said with annoyance, "do you want to sell me this car or don't you?"

"Sure . . . sure," was the reluctant answer.

The photographer gave the salesman a fifty dollar deposit on the $2,280.50 car; a week later he was advised that the car was ready to be picked up. With a cashier's check in hand, he returned to the showroom to complete the transaction. The salesman began to shuffle papers on his desk.

"We have a little problem here. Your car was originally ordered by a customer who wanted a number of extras. He never took delivery, but I still have to charge you for the extras."

"How much?" the photographer demanded.

The salesman did some fast figuring. "It comes to $124.80."

The photographer paid for the "extras" because he

needed the car immediately. He suspected there were actually no extras—a suspicion confirmed a few weeks later by a friend in the automobile business. The charges had simply been tacked on to make up for the lost finance charges.

Senator Douglas' Subcommittee hearings invited the testimony of Herbert E. Cheever, Vice President of the First National Bank in Brookings, S. Dakota. Mr. Cheever told the Subcommittee:

"Most installment lending departments in banks as well as finance companies will give the [automobile] dealers approximately 20 per cent of the finance fee for originating and selling them the business. Some finance companies will even pay the dealer a percentage of the insurance premium which, of course, creates earnings for the dealer but likewise has a tendency to increase finance costs of the unsuspecting. This is one of the things that creates excessive credit costs."

A Sioux Falls case was read into the record by the U.S. Employees Federal Credit Union of that city. It involved one of its members, who purchased a four-door Chevrolet sport coupe which, with accessories, came to $3,049.29. He was allowed $1,074.28 in trade for his 1952 Pontiac, $629 of which went to a finance company to pay off the outstanding balance on the old automobile.

The difference, plus a $300 cash deposit, left a balance due of $2,304 on the new car. Insurance premiums totalling $108.50 were added along with a time price differential of $355.02. This figure apparently represented the finance cost on the loan.

The car buyer then signed a conditional sales contract in the amount of $2,767.52, payable in eleven monthly installments of $75, and one final payment of $1,020.02. This contract was assigned by the automobile dealer to a local finance company.

Because of the final "balloon" payment in the note, it is next to impossible to determine the true interest rate on this loan. Presumably, the loan was intended to be renewed annually, with a new time price differential added each time. It would be hard to predict what the finance charges would have been over the total life of this loan, but judging from the first year's cost of $355.02, one can surmise that they would have been substantial.

Fortunately for the car owner, the Sioux Falls U.S. Employees Federal Credit Union refinanced the balance due on his loan at the end of the first year, and he was spared the painful experience of finding out just how much his loan would cost to liquidate.

Dr. Theodore O. Yntema, Vice-President in charge of finance for the Ford Motor Company, summed up the situation when he told the Committee:

"The variety and complexity of finance and insurance arrangements and the charges for them are such as almost to defy comprehension. It is impossible for the average buyer to appraise the rates."

The hearings conducted by Senator Douglas extended over a period of three years; the record runs to thousands of cases. As a result of Committee findings, Senator Douglas, on February 7, 1963, introduced his "Truth-in-Lending" Bill. This legislation would require that all lenders and credit sellers fully disclose to the consumer "the cost of using credit in an accurate and uniform manner."

And what is happening to the Truth-in-Lending bill? Nothing. Nineteen senators in the 88th Congress joined Senator Douglas in pushing for the legislation, but the opposition from finance company lobbies has been formidable—and the bill does not have the kind of White House support it needs to counter this opposition. Explains a top governmental official: "The main reason the Truth-in-Lending Bill hasn't gone through is that the ordinary consumer doesn't have a $100,000-a-year lobby in back of him."

Auto financing has been the object of scrutiny in other than federal circles. The results of a study conducted at the University of California at Berkeley were published recently in the *Journal of Home Economics.* Some families, the survey found, were paying interest rates as high as 110 per cent to finance the purchase of used cars.

"Many of the families studied could undoubtedly have saved on the finance charges if they had shopped for credit as ardently as they shopped for their cars," the report declared. "However, almost four-fifths of them did not check any source of credit other than through car dealers.

"The advantage to be gained by shopping for credit was revealed by the fact that those who had shopped for credit for used cars paid a median rate of 12 per cent, compared with 22.9 per cent paid by those who had not shopped. "The majority were under the impression they were paying a rate of 5 or 6 per cent."

Few of the families surveyed were even aware that car dealers *make a profit on the installment contract as well as on the car.* This is possible because the finance charge is determined by the dealer who writes the contract, *not* by the financial institution to which the monthly payments are made.

"If a dealer reduces his profit on a car, or increases the trade-in allowance, he will probably increase his profit on the finance charge," according to the *Journal of Home Economics* article. "For example, one automobile salesman explained that his dealer's anticipated profit was $800 on the make of car he was selling. However, salesmen were permitted to allow as much as a $600 discount, providing the dealer arranged for the financing.

"When a maximum $600 discount was given, an 'add-on' or contract rate of 9 per cent was charged instead of the usual add-on rate of 6.5 per cent. On a three-year installment contract a 9 per cent add-on rate results in simple interest rate of 17.5 per cent, where a 6.5 per cent rate gives a 12.7 per cent simple interest rate."

Small wonder that not everything's clear to the car owner.

The alarming degree to which auto retailing has become a financing con game was clearly revealed in California recently. At a hearing before California's Corporation Commissioner, Sears, Roebuck & Co. placed its request for a license to go into the automobile loan business.

Sears' reason for wanting to make auto loans was no dark secret. A part of the company's vast merchandising empire is Allstate Insurance Co., the largest seller of auto insurance in the country, which then operated in 23 other states. In California, Sears made plain its intention to offer car loans at rates that would be below those available from most other lenders. Established lenders and car dealers immediately pooled their considerable lobby power into a drive on the Corporations Commissioner to deny Sears a license. The concerted lobby effort succeeded in delaying a decision on the Sears application, made in July 1964, for week after week. Finally, in October, the Corporations Commissioner called for a hearing on the matter, an unusual procedure in the granting of such licenses.

It was quite a hearing. Banks, small loan companies, industrial loan companies, sales finance companies, independent insurance companies, and auto dealers were all there, as well as Sears, of course. A big pot was at stake. More than 10 per cent of all cars sold—new and used, for cash or credit—are bought in California, where auto sales in 1965 totaled about $4 billion. An estimated 70 per cent of that amount is being financed at rates ranging upward of 36 per cent true annual interest to a low of around 8 per cent.

Among those called upon to testify at the hearing was Gil Ashcom, president of the Northern California Motor Car Dealers Association.

"May I ask you one question, Mr. Ashcom? Do you want to sell cars for cash?"

"I do not want to sell them for cash if I can avoid it."

"You would not want to sell the cars you do for a cash price then?"

"No, sir."

"Does this mean that you are not really in the business of selling automobiles?"

"It does not mean that at all."

"But you do not want to sell automobiles for cash?"

"It means that I want to sell cars for the most profit that I can per car. Finance reserve [dealer's share of the carrying charges] and insurance commissions are part of the profit derived from selling a car on time."

It wasn't until February 1965 that a ruling was handed down, and Allstate was allowed to operate in California.

It was the Consumer Court of California which recently issued the following guide for use in determining true interest charges when the debt is paid in one year:

When they say	*You actually pay*
4% per year:	7.3%
6% per year:	10.9%
8% per year:	14.5%
10% per year:	18.0%
1% per month:	21.5%

. . . If interest is charged "only on the unpaid balance":

When they say	*You actually pay*
3/4 of 1% per month:	9%
5/6 of 1% per month:	10%
1% per month:	12%
1 and ¼% per month:	15%
1 and ½% per month:	18%
2 and ½% per month:	30%

Dealers who gyp customers in the financing of cars are not, of course, confined to the West Coast. This case was reported to the Better Business Bureau in an eastern seaboard city:

A widow with two children had a late model two-door sedan which she wanted to trade in on a station wagon. In a used car lot one afternoon just before closing time, she found one that suited her needs exactly.

"With my trade-in, how much is it going to cost me?" she asked.

"Seven hundred and fifty dollars. Only $59.66 a month."

The arrangement sounded reasonable and she agreed. There was just one problem. "The office help has gone home for the day," the salesman said. "However, I have all the papers we'll need. So that you won't have to come back, just sign them and I'll have a copy mailed to you tomorrow as soon as they're filled out."

A few days later the unsuspecting woman received the papers. As she read the no-longer blank contract she had signed, the poor woman could scarcely believe her eyes. Instead of the anticipated $750 she now owed a total of $1,116.

After she reported the case to the Better Business Bureau, an investigator found these extra items added to the contract without her consent or knowledge:

- A health and accident policy at $55.80

- A credit life insurance policy at $22.32

- An "investigative fee" of $21

- An unidentified item amounting to $28.43

And there was a finance charge of 10 per cent amounting to $101.45.

If you're a prospective car owner, bear these guidelines in mind:

1. If you can't afford to pay at least one-third down, perhaps you should buy a less expensive car. If you finance too much of the purchase price, you'll soon wind up owing more than the market value of the car.

2. You don't have to finance your car through the dealer who sold it to you. Remember, he usually gets a hefty premium from the finance company that supplies the money to handle financing. Shop for credit. Try your local bank.

3. If you have doubts, consult someone in whom you have confidence: your banker, lawyer, insurance agent, or the Better Business Bureau.

4. Never, under any circumstances, sign a blank contract.

5. Before you sign any papers, read the small print. Ask as many questions as necessary to clarify the deal in your own mind.

6. Obtain a copy of all papers you sign. Be sure they are identical with the originals, and approved by the manager—not just a salesman.

CHAPTER VII

Insurance: accidentally on purpose

THE SUN GLISTENED on the chrome of the sleek new Cadillac as it swept down a highway that cut through the rolling countryside of Pennsylvania. Inside, the owner of a large chain of hardware stores sat relaxed at the wheel, his thoughts drifting from the road ahead to the details of a business meeting that was taking him to Harrisburg, just five miles away. A stop light ahead turned red and he automatically slowed. Had his mind not been on business, he might have paid more attention to a battered old car that rattled past him and stopped at the light. He pulled up behind the jalopy and waited.

When the light turned green, the first car started

forward again. The Cadillac followed. Then, suddenly, without warning, the ancient vehicle stopped short. The hardware man hit his brakes—but it was too late. The Cadillac rammed into the back of the other car.

The Cadillac owner remembers all four doors of the other car flying open and, as he told state troopers later, "Four people came spinning out like oranges, screaming. All I could think was that I had done something awful."

Then, he recalls, a man crawled over to him on hands and knees and cried out: "You almost killed my family!"

Two ambulances arrived a short time later and all five passengers were rushed to a local hospital. The dazed owner of the Cadillac managed to find a phone and call his insurance company. Guiltily he recited the facts to an adjuster. It was merely another routine accident report until the hardware man began to describe the unfortunate victims. "They looked like a bunch of gypsies," he said.

There was a long moment of silence at the other end of the line. "Gypsies? Are you sure?"

The hardware man was sure. "Why do you ask?"

"Just a hunch. You'll hear from us." Then the adjuster added: "Don't discuss the accident with anybody."

The adjuster telephoned the New York City headquarters of the American Insurance Association, watchdog of the insurance industry, which represents more than 200 stock and mutual insurance firms. He spoke to Robert W. Dick, assistant claims manager and a former

FBI agent. Dick listened, and then, "This may be the break we've been looking for," he said. "I'll send an agent down there immediately. Thanks for calling."

Dick's and the adjuster's intuition paid off. When the AIA investigator arrived in Harrisburg, he tagged the driver of the battered car as a notorious gypsy often called "Big Pig," although he operated under any one of at least fifteen different aliases. The gypsy's record filled almost an entire drawer of a police file cabinet. In this instance, "Big Pig" had had along as passengers his wife, their seventeen-year-old son, and the boy's girl friend. All were questioned by both the AIA agent and the local police. The authorities made no real progress toward proving fraud until they concentrated on the girl friend. She confessed that the boy had promised to give her a new dress, perfume and other gifts. "But," she said, "I never got anything."

As the investigators continued to question the girl, she made other references to broken promises. Bit by bit her resistance weakened and she finally blurted out: "They all deserve to be punished. I'll tell you what *really* happened!"

The Harrisburg accident, she confessed, had been rigged. She described how the group had cruised the highway looking for a "mark." When they spotted the new Cadillac, "Big Pig" drove in front of it and deliberately slammed on the brakes. "After the car hit us, we piled out and went into our act," she explained. "We weren't really even bruised."

The gypsy, his wife, and their son were arrested and indicted for attempted insurance fraud. They pleaded guilty and each was given a year in jail.

The penalty seems light when one considers the special AIA report prepared later. "The group specialized in rear-end automobile accidents," it read. "Almost always they selected expensive cars. Their own cars were picked up for $25 or less. They would maneuver in front of other vehicles—stop suddenly and unpredictably—thus causing the other automobile to strike them. Under the law, in most circumstances, the car in the rear would be liable. Invariably, at the scene of the accident, they would demand that an ambulance be called. When the insurance adjuster arrived at the hospital, they would go into a well-rehearsed routine, writhing in agony. As soon as the adjuster left, a miraculous recovery would take place. They would be discharged before the day was out."

The gypsies would then press for a quick settlement, giving an out-of-state address and saying that they were required to return home promptly. The AIA found that the family had filed a total of 33 claims over a period of five years in such cities as Providence, Bridgeport, New York and Philadelphia—in addition to two in Harrisburg. Known settlements amounted to $23,000. Not bad for the little effort involved.

The rear-end collision gimmick made even bigger money for a gang which was finally caught up with in Cleveland. Members of the ring had made 37 claims involving staged accidents throughout the Middle West. Each started with a deliberate rear-end collision. Said the report that followed: "There were duplicate medical bills and property damage estimates. They would exchange drivers, use several aliases, switch identities, and use numerous cars with fictitious registrations."

Not long ago a quite different, and particularly gruesome, scheme was uncovered on the West Coast. The plan, devised by a bartender, involved himself, his wife and a chiropractor friend. The plot called for the bartender's car (empty) to be sideswiped and knocked over a cliff by the chiropractor's car (heavily-insured). The bartender would be found beside his wrecked automobile with fractures of the arm and leg. His wife would be found unconscious. The bartender's injuries were to be deliberately inflicted by his chiropractor friend; the wife would be knocked unconscious by drugs.

Los Angeles' Coliseum Park, on a June night, was picked for the scene of the staged accident. The conspirators appeared in three cars—one of which was to be used for the getaway. First, the chiropractor gave the bartender a hypodermic to deaden the pain that would come from later ministrations. The drugged wife had already fallen into the intended coma. Everything was set. The chiropractor took a firm grip on the bartender's arm and had just broken it with a sharp crack when a searchlight stabbed the darkness.

"Hold it!" a voice commanded. The pair, with the bartender in genuine agony, turned to find a Los Angeles Police Department radio car parked a short distance away. An officer stepped out, walked over and placed the two men and the unconscious woman under arrest.

The trio was taken to the County Sheriff's Department for questioning. The pained bartender insisted, "We haven't done anything wrong." A burly deputy sheriff snapped back: "We've been watching all three of you for the past month. We knew you were up to something when you doubled the insurance on one of your cars." What the deputy sheriff didn't say was that the case had really been broken through information supplied by the chiropractor's telephone receptionist.

In Philadelphia recently, the District Attorney charged that a highly organized gang had registered a 1959 Plymouth in New Jersey, under a fictitious name, and had then proceeded to arrange a series of "three-car collisions" at different locations. For the damaged Plymouth, claims were submitted to four different insurance carriers. Explanation of the "accident" in each case included mention that the other two cars involved had been driven off the scene by their respective owners.

What eventually tripped up these crooks was their own laziness. In submitting one claim, they didn't bother to retype, but simply sent the insurance company a carbon copy of the claim they had submitted elsewhere before. This piece of stupidity touched off a full-scale investigation. It was found that all checks issued by the insurance companies for claim payments were cashed through a single body repair shop. Seventeen persons were cited for their involvement in the scheme, which had defrauded insurance companies of over $100,000.

Morgan Woods, manager of the AIA Claims Bureau, says that three out of every four auto insurance claims are "tainted with some element of fraud." Far from all of it is the work of organized gangs. A young woman in Manhasset, Long Island, alleged injury when the car she was driving was struck. She claimed a loss of ten weeks work at a salary of $125 a week. As "proof" she submitted a letter from her employer and one from her doctor. When the insurance money ($1,067.50) came through she used it to go on a honeymoon.

A jealous friend tipped off the insurance company, which got the AIA onto the case. Investigation showed that the accident had been staged with the help of the girl's fiancée—and that the letters from her employer and doctor had been forged. The young woman was indicted and convicted of grand larceny.

Then there was Robert Mitzner, an Oklahoma salesman who was having trouble meeting the monthly finance payments on his car. It all started when the windshield cracked—a minor misfortune that gave Mitzner his big idea. The AIA report explains: "His scheme was to stop a truck loaded with rocks or gravel and complain that when the truck had passed him on the road a mile or so back a rock had fallen out and smashed his windshield. Mitzner would obtain the name of the trucker's insurance company and present a claim."

Eventually, insurance companies that had been hit more than once with his claims asked the AIA to investigate. They turned up a total of 37 broken windshield claims presented by him. Indicted and tried in

Seminole County, Oklahoma, he got a two-year jail sentence.

Although the average American finds "larceny" an ugly word when it is applied to him, that is exactly what cheating an insurance company amounts to. The small and large frauds perpetuated by American motorists add up to a fantastic figure. "We estimate that it is in excess of $350,000,000 a year," says Mr. Woods of the AIA Claims Bureau. In that same single year, the amount of auto-accident claims—both legitimate and phony—for personal injury and property damage totaled *four billion dollars.*

"It isn't simply that millions of car-owners are cheats," says Woods. "Many honest people just allow themselves to get involved in these situations. They get an over-assessment from the garage, and then receive an over-evaluation of the claim from their lawyer. The notion grows that they can obtain a good deal of money by stretching the truth and filing a lawsuit. The lawyer agrees to take a retainer and in many instances, merely goes through the motions of filing, even though he knows the case has no merit. Eventually the case will be settled out of court. And who pays? Every motorist who carries an automobile insurance policy—through higher premiums."

In so many cases, it happens as this did: Jack and Nora Hill were spending a pleasant Sunday house-hunting. Driving along a parkway on the outskirts of New York City, Nora saw the sign: "New Development . . . Model House Open." So Jack stepped on the brake as he prepared to turn off at the next exit. Suddenly he was hit from behind, and his car bounced off the road.

Though Jack and Nora were both dazed, neither was seriously hurt. The driver of the other car, all apologies, exchanged license registration and insurance information with Jack. The incident was too minor to call the police. It ended with a handshake.

At home, Jack called an attorney acquaintance and explained what happened. The attorney advised: "Now do exactly what I say. Discuss this case with no one. Stay home from work tomorrow. Tell the office you were in an automobile accident and are in pain. I'll take care of all the details."

"What about Nora?" Jack asked.

"Tell her to report for work as usual. Then, after an hour, have her see the company nurse and complain of dizziness and headache."

Following the script, the nurse sent Nora home, making note of it in her employment file.

After Jack had called his office to say, "I have to see my doctor because of the accident," he presented himself, on the attorney's instructions, at the office of a Dr. Wilton. The doctor gave him a ten-minute check-up, took a simple X-ray, and informed Jack that a complete medical report would be sent to his attorney. Nora was also sent to see the doctor, for the same brief examination and an X-ray. Both she and Jack were told to inform their employers that they were receiving medical treatment, and would be out for at least a week.

The attorney then filed suit against the other driver, seeking damages for medical bills, damage to the car, and what is known as "loss of consortium" (loss of Nora's services as a wife). Jack's X-rays showed that he had suffered "bruised thoracic vertebrae." The examination report also indicated that Nora suffered from violent headaches and a "severe nervous condition."

If Nora or Jack had any pangs of conscience, they were eliminated by the lawyer's observation: "Everybody does it."

Negotiations began with the attorney for the insurance company; a compromise was sought. If a settlement wasn't worked out it could be years before the case came to trial—an average of four years in New York City, as against five in Chicago, three in Boston. Jack was also aware that the insurance company's trial attorney might tear down his entire case, with the jury ruling for the insurance company.

From the insurance company's point of view, considering the astronomical awards by benevolent juries, an out-of-court settlement was probably the least expensive solution—despite the fact that the insurance attorney suspected Jack's case was a weak one.

Jack was claiming an amount in excess of $850—the average in auto accidents where personal injuries are involved. The insurance attorney balked—$850, yes; $1,250, no. He warned Jack that he would be interrogated in court by a trial attorney who specialized in "shaking" witnesses on the stand. There was a meeting at which the trial attorney sized up Jack. Afterwards, he advised his company: "Settle. The plaintiff would be a tough witness on the stand."

A few days later, Jack's lawyer telephoned to report that the case had finally been settled for $950. When the check was mailed to the lawyer, he deducted his fee, the doctor's fees, and "miscellaneous expenses." What did Jack and Nora end up with? A check for $400. Jack was incensed. "I should never have started. It wasn't worth all that aggravation. Everybody made money except us!"

The one injury which leads to most fraud in auto accident claims is something called "whiplash." The term was originally coined in 1928 by a Los Angeles orthopedic surgeon, Dr. Harold E. Crowe, who is still in practice. He used the word to describe what had caused the condition of eight patients who, through auto accidents, suffered neck injuries which proved difficult to cure. Dr. Crowe referred to the condition in an address before the American Academy of Medicine. Since then, he has lived to regret the term—and so have the insurance companies.

"The expression was intended to be a description of motion—not of a disease," Dr. Crowe said recently.

The term whiplash caught on with doctors, patients and claimants' attorneys. It is now almost a household word. Nearly nine out of every ten persons involved in an accident in which one car hits another car from behind develop this very popular "disease."

Dr. Crowe and other medical experts take the view that actual "whiplash" is extremely rare. To support his contention, Dr. Crowe delivered a paper before an American Bar Association convention, citing the results of some 300 cases for which he examined hospital records over a three-year period. He found that only 18 of the 300 victims of whiplash would actually have benefited from medical treatment. "The remaining 282 patients had suffered from simple strains which would have been cured if left entirely alone," Dr. Crowe stated.

In many cases of rear-end accidents, he pointed out, the victim is convinced he must have a neck injury and *thinks* himself into it. Psychiatrists agree with him.

In a speech before the Western Orthopedic Association at San Francisco, Dr. Crowe suggested that a "green poultice" is the best cure for most whiplash cases. "By 'green poultice' I mean a financial settlement," he said wryly. "There's no question but what such a settlement has a high therapeutic value. Insurance claims adjusters have known for years that 'whiplash' victims get well with amazing rapidity after they receive their court settlements."

Many doctors have found "green poultices" soothing to them, too. Two years ago in Miami, a Dr. Shirley was questioned by an attorney during the course of a Circuit Court case.

Q. "What are some of the ailments from which your patients suffer?"

A. "Many suffer from cervical sprains."

Q. "You mean whiplash?"

A. "That is correct."

Q. "How many whiplash cases would you say you have treated?"

A. "Are you talking about the past year or since I have been in practice?"

Q. "Since you have been in practice."

A. "I would say 3,000 cases. I have as many as 300 or 400 going currently." (Dr. Shirley had begun his Florida practice in 1957.)

Later cross-examination uncovered the fact that 90 to 95 per cent of the cases Dr. Shirley handled involved automobile accidents. The attorney told the jury that the doctor's average fee was $411. At that rate, he pointed out, Dr. Shirley's 3,000 cases would have earned him $1,233,000!

The practice of filing exaggerated claims, as it became widespread, led to the formation of an association which has been called "a school for insurance larceny": the National Association of Claimants' Compensation Attorneys. The NACCA, formed in the late fifties, now has 15,000 members; its avowed purpose is to "protect clients." Member lawyers are said to attend regular seminars at which experts tutor them in the art of dramatizing a client's injuries.

Philip H. Corboy is the NACCA's president. To the insurance companies' suggestion that many claims for injuries are exaggerated, Corboy responds:

"What the insurance companies flatly refuse to accept is that the law allows recovery for something more than doctors' bills and hospital bills and loss of earnings.

"Pain and suffering, terms of anathema to the stoics in the ivory towers of the insurance companies, are compensable damages under our law.

"These corporate executives would prefer to dictatorially conclude that but a small amount of money should be granted for this legitimate factor."

As for the insurance industry's assertion that it is losing money on auto insurance underwriting, Corboy says:

"That's ridiculous! The so-called loss is the result of competent accountants utilizing a system wherein profits on investments do not show up on the underwriting department's ledger."

Corboy cites a U.S. Department of Labor survey showing that of every dollar in premiums, only 43 cents is paid out to claimants and 57 cents goes to overhead and profits.

"In figuring the rates," he says, "the companies do not consider the investment income they earn."

Insurance companies counter that they are not in the investment business. They say the profit from investment of their reserves is necessary to protect policy owners and claimants.

Corboy says he and his NACCA colleagues have no quarrel with the insurance industry's legitimate pursuit of profits.

"We do quarrel, however, with the smoke screen precipitated in the guise of an attack on the contingent fee system, an attack on the jury system and an accusation that 'phony' claims are the cause of raises in premium rates."

All of the NACCA's arguments come under sharp attack from the legal profession itself.

Josh H. Groce of San Antonio, Texas, one of the country's leading defense attorneys, said at the 24th annual meeting of the Federation of Insurance Counsel:

"The defense cause is for the fair and impartial trials where justice is administered according to rules of evidence and not thwarted by inflammatory, demonstrative evidence used for the purpose of swaying the jury to prejudicial decisions.

"The defense cause is for the prompt settlement of legitimate claims—those claims which have real injuries and in which there are questions of liability. The cause is against compensation of faked injuries such as 'whiplash' or those other catch-all injuries which are used to cover up feigned injuries or exaggerate others. The defense cause is against the use of medical treatments which actually aggravate rather than cure the patient. *The defense cause is for honest and truthful medical testimony.* It challenges the integrity of those doctors who testify on the basis of compensation rather than on their examination."

Honesty and truth serve the individual car owner well, too. For it is obvious that in our attempts to extract large sums from insurance companies, we are only defrauding ourselves—because we all pay the bill through higher premium rates.

To protect yourself, one leading insurance company suggests:

1. If you are borrowing money to buy your car, the

lender has the right to require you to carry enough insurance to protect the car from collision or other damage. Often, your car dealer will offer you auto insurance for this purpose. Before you buy it, make sure you won't be paying too much by checking with a few insurance agents or, at least, the agent you already have.

2. While the lender is vitally interested in seeing that you have collision coverage to protect his investment, he is not so interested in making sure you have liability protection. *Be sure you have it.* If you drive your new car off the lot without adequate liability protection, you may be making the costliest mistake of your life. An adverse judgment in a personal injury case can cost you more than every car you'll ever buy.

And remember, finally, that:

3. Filing an exaggerated claim only means that everybody but you is going to make money. If it's something minor, don't get involved with a lawyer—talk directly with the insurance company.

CHAPTER VIII

How should you be covered—and how much should you pay?

FOR HIS OWN PROTECTION against being "taken" in the area of insurance buying—oversold, undersold, overcharged, or misinformed—the average car owner needs to keep in mind a few basic guide-lines. At the very least, these will save important dollars year after year.

The Insurance Information Institute lists six basic areas of coverage in which every driver needs protection:

1. *Bodily injury liability insurance.* This coverage applies when your car injures or kills pedestrians, persons riding in other cars, or passengers in your own car. It is in force as long as your car is driven by you, mem-

bers of your immediate family, or others who drive your car with your permission. You and all members of your family are covered even while driving someone else's car if you have the owner's permission. If a claim or suit is brought against you, insurance provides protection in the form of legal defense, and if it is agreed or judged by a court that you are legally liable, the insuring company will pay damages assessed against you up to the limits of the policy.

2. *Property damage liability insurance.* This coverage applies when your car damages the property of others. More often than not the property involved is another car; but it also covers damages to such other properties as lamp posts, telephone poles, or buildings. Again, you and all members of your family are covered even while driving someone else's car if you have the owner's permission. And, as with bodily injury insurance, this coverage provides protection in the form of legal defense.

3. *Medical payments insurance.* Under this coverage the insuring company agrees to pay, up to the limits of the policy, medical expenses resulting from accidental injury. Payment does not depend on litigation. It applies to you and your immediate family whether in their car, someone else's, or if struck while walking. It applies to passengers who occupy your automobile. *Payment is made regardless of who is at fault, or even if no one is at fault.* Such insurance is a must if you share a car pool,

or if your wife hauls a carload of children to and from school.

4. *Protection against uninsured motorist.* Coverage here applies to bodily injuries for which an uninsured motorist, or a hit-and-run driver, is legally liable. It applies to the policy holder and his family whether occupying their car, someone else's, or while walking. It also applies to passengers in your car. Damages are paid to injured persons to the same extent that they would have been paid if the uninsured or unknown motorist had carried insurance.

5. *Comprehensive insurance.* This means protection against financial loss resulting from breakage of glass, falling objects, fire, theft of car, explosion, earthquake, windstorm, hail, water, flood, vandalism or malicious mischief, riot or civil commotion, or collision with a bird or animal. But it does not cover personal possessions stolen from a car. For this you need what is known as a "floater" policy.

6. *Collision insurance.* This coverage applies when your car is damaged as a result of colliding with a vehicle or other object, or as a result of turning over. Damages are paid by the insuring company regardless of who is at fault. Most collision insurance is sold on a $50 to $100 deductible basis. This means that the car owner agrees to pay the first $50 or $100 of damage to his car in any one collision, and the insuring company pays the balance.

Collision insurance does not cover injuries to people or damage to the property of others.

Along with the cost of practically everything else in life, that of automobile insurance has kept going up and up. The reasons are clear: there are more cars, more accidents; higher repair costs; more people making claims; larger court awards for personal injuries. In the last ten years, auto-insurance companies have paid out over $850,000,000 on bodily-injury policies. As a result, motor-vehicle liability insurance has jumped over 50 per cent!

	LOS ANGELES		*CHICAGO*		*PHILADELPHIA*	
	10 years ago	*Today*	*10 years ago*	*Today*	*10 years ago*	*Today*
Liability *	$105	$172	$124	$192	$140	$207
Collision ($100 deductible)	$ 32	$ 86	$ 34	$ 72	$118	$156
Compre-hensive	$ 28	$ 47	$ 20	$ 57	$ 24	$ 61
Total:	$165	$305	$178	$321	$282	$424

* Liability coverage is 10/20/5. (This means a policy which provides for maximum payment of $10,000 for one person injured or killed; $20,000 for two or more persons injured or killed; $5,000 for property damage.)

Note: Figures apply to a couple with a 17-year-old, driving a four-door standard sedan. *Source:* National Automobile Underwriters Association, National Bureau of Casualty Underwiters.

The price you pay is regulated by state authorities. They examine statistics on claims prepared by insurance companies, and then determine whether the rates to be charged are fair. The fact that rates are regulated by state authorities does not mean, however, that all companies must charge the same premiums, offer exactly the same coverages, or render the same services. All firms are free to compete in terms of price, coverage, and service.

As is obvious from the chart above, basic rates for automobile insurance are not the same throughout the country. States are divided into "rating territories" for determining rates. A territory may be a city, a part of a city, a suburb, or a rural area. For each territory, insurance companies compile statistics on claims resulting from bodily injury or property damage and base their rates on this "loss experience."

Aside from the *amount* of coverage you want to buy, there are other factors that are considered in the cost: driver classification, which is based on age, sex, marital status, how you use your car, and your driving record; driver education, which applies to young drivers; the limits of protection you choose for certain coverages; the deductive clause; and the year, make, and model of your car.

Can you do anything about cutting the cost of your insurance? The answer is a heartening yes: more than 250 companies affiliated with the National Bureau of Casualty Underwriters and the National Automobile Underwriters Association have worked out various discounts which enable motorists to reduce their premiums. Here are eight ways of saving money:

Safe driver insurance plans

These plans are in effect in most states. Under such a plan, if you, and everyone in the family who drives your car, have had clear driving records during the past 3 years, you get a discount off your basic premiums for liability and collision insurance. The discount is 10, 15 or 20 per cent, depending upon the state. A "clear driving record" means not having been involved in an accident that was your fault, and not having been convicted of any serious traffic law violation. According to current figures, more than 70 per cent of American motorists can qualify for a safe driver discount.

(On the other hand, if you or other drivers in your family have been responsible for accidents or have been convicted of serious traffic violations, you pay 5 to 150 per cent more than the basic premiums. The plan works on a point system: the more points you accumulate due to accidents and convictions, the more you pay.)

Special economy policy

Available in most states, this is a "package" policy that offers liability, medical payments, collision, and comprehensive insurance at a lower cost than the same coverages if brought separately. The savings range from 10 to 20 per cent, depending upon the state.

Compact car discount

If you own a 1955 or later model domestic or foreign "compact" passenger car, not classified as a "sports car," it's possible to get a 10 per cent discount on automobile liability and collision insurance premiums. Your car cannot exceed (a) a list price of $2,750, (b) 125 braking horsepower, (c) 3,000 pounds in manufacturer's specified weight, or d) 200 inches in over-all length.

Discount for two or more cars

If you own two or more private passenger cars, you may qualify for a discount off your liability and collision insurance premiums, provided both cars are covered by the same company.

Driver education discount

If a driver under 21 in your household has successfully completed a course in driver education, you may be eligible for a discount. Driver education courses must meet the standards set by the National Commission on Safety Education of the National Education Association. More than 10,000 high schools and colleges throughout the country provide courses which meet these standards and are recognized as qualifying for the discount.

Farmer discount

If you are engaged in farming or ranching you can qualify for a discount on your private passenger cars, station wagons, and jeep-type automobiles. (Farmers' trucks with a load capacity of 1,500 pounds or less are regarded as private passenger cars.) To qualify for the discount, a "farm automobile" must be one which is principally garaged on a farm or ranch and is not customarily used in going to or from work other than farming or ranching and is not used in any occupation other than farming or ranching.

Non-resident student discount

In many states, parents of young drivers who live at schools which are more than 100 miles from the place of principal garaging of the automobile, can qualify for a 10 per cent premium discount, since such students are only part-of-the-year drivers.

Discount for women aged 30 to 64

If she is the only one in the home who drives the car, a woman 30 through 64 years of age is usually eligible for a 10 per cent premium discount.

If you can qualify for one or more of these discounts, consult your insurance agent or broker.

One last tip on auto insurance: it rarely pays to cut corners. Don't try to out-think your insurance agent—be guided by his advice.

CHAPTER IX

The tow-car haul

A. O. CREWS was a salesman from Memphis, Tennessee, headed south for Florida. Late in the afternoon, he entered the city of Pensacola. Suddenly, a car darted from the right out of an intersection. He slammed on his brakes, but it was too late. The car smashed into the right side of his Buick.

An hour later Crews stood facing a police captain in Pensacola Police Headquarters. His head was covered with a blood-soaked bandage applied by an ambulance attendant at the scene of the accident; he was under arrest; his car was a wreck; and he was nearly three hundred miles from home.

The captain glanced up from the police blotter. "Bail is one hundred dollars—cash."

"Will you take a check?" Crews asked.

"No checks."

Crews, hurt and bewildered, asked if he could make a phone call.

"One only," the captain said.

Crews put in a collect call to a friend in Memphis, but was advised: "We're sorry, sir, your party is out of town."

As Crews turned away from the phone, the police captain asked casually. "Where's your car now?"

"There was a wrecker at the scene," Crews told him. "He towed it to his garage. Said he was going to fix it."

"What was the name of the garage?" the captain asked.

"It was an outfit called Murphy Brothers," Crews said.

The captain looked genuinely concerned. "That's too bad," he said, "the Murphy Brothers will rob you blind. You're in for a lot of trouble if you leave the car with them."

Then a funny thing happened, which the captain later told a grand jury was a "coincidence." A man appeared, wearing a garageman's uniform. On the back, bold red letters announced: "FREDDIE'S GARAGE." And in smaller letters: "Wrecks Repaired Day and Night."

The captain called the garageman over. Then he turned to Crews and said, "You're really in luck. Here's the best body-and-fender man in Pensacola. You've got nothing to worry about. He's one of my police officers. He'll take good care of you."

The captain paused for a moment to let the point sink in. Then, he said, "Now, on the question of your bond. Since my man is going to handle the repair job, I'll reduce the bail to $10."

Crews paid up. And let Freddie, the moonlighting cop, repair the car. But, unlike most victimized motorists, Crews didn't take it lying down. He let out his anger in a letter to the American Automobile Association, describing exactly what had happened. It was his letter that lowered the boom.

A. Ridgely Jones, vice-president of the Pensacola Motor Club, said later: "We had received a number of complaints from motorists who had had similar experiences with the Pensacola police. But for the first time, with Crews' letter, we had something we could really work on. We organized a special task force of AAA members from other areas and moved in. The local authorities fought us all the way—we even had cops tailing us. But we wouldn't throw in the towel. Finally, we forced the case into the grand jury."

The results were a page-one story for days. Seventeen police officers and two tow-car operators were indicted. Grand jury evidence disclosed that the Pensacola tow-car racket was costing motorists $1,000,000 a year. An attractive young widow, Mrs. Lois Sheffield, who had taken over the running of her husband's garage after his death, testified that there were forty-five police officers on her payroll. She produced records to show that in a single year her garage had spent $4,000 as "payola" just to lure wreckage-call business to her firm. The standard fee paid to police officers ran from ten to twenty dollars for each tow job "turned over." Her charges were backed up by numerous affidavits produced by the AAA.

The Pensacola Police Department was subsequently re-organized from top to bottom. A number of police officers resigned, including Police Chief Crosby Hall, who told the grand jury: "I am aware that some of my men are on the take. But what can I do about it?"

The Pensacola scandal is just a case in point. The tow-car racket exists in all fifty states of the Union. Only recently in Alaska there was a monumental uproar when a motorist, who had been marooned in a snowbank, was charged $425.10 to be hauled back to civilization.

According to authorities, car-towing costs the motoring public about $150,000,000 a year. Morgan Woods, head of the claims department of the American Insurance Association, watchdog of the insurance industry, says: "Despite the many crackdowns, collusion between police and tow-car operators continues to flourish. Their particular victim is the motorist whose car is in an accident or breaks down far away from home. The tow-car operators move in like vultures. The ones who get the business, in many cases, are those who have the best police connections."

In Chicago, charges of graft and thievery have been part of the Windy City's hoist-'em-and-haul-'em business almost since there were enough autos for one to collide with another. Its biggest scandal broke some years ago.

Virgil W. Peterson, the Chicago Crime Commission's operating director, painted a grim picture of rival tow trucks racing one another to the scene of an accident. Here are some of his findings, from a report prepared by the Commission:

- "Racketeers, working rapidly and brazenly in an aura of bribery at the scene of auto accidents, compound the heartbreak of the victims."

- "The racketeers strike at every motorist—in that their activities are a factor causing auto-insurance rates to rise. They collect huge fees in what has become a multi-million-dollar business . . ."

- "Some policemen and tow-truck drivers dicker over payoffs even as ambulances are carrying away the injured and motorists lie dead in the street."

Special agent R. C. Chapman of the Chicago office of the AIA wrote in a confidential report to headquarters: "The police officer got twelve dollars in cash for reporting each job. If it was an old model, the fee would be five dollars. Then there would be a percentage of the repair bill. For every call received, the garage would note on its books the squad-car number and make a circle in red around it."

The Chicago probe produced testimony to prove

that claim adjusters submitted to exorbitant charges for towing in order to escape even higher repair charges.

"We pay as much as fifty dollars to some tow garages to regain possession of cars after accidents," one insurance claim agent admitted. "They add all sorts of handling charges to the original fee. But it's worth it if further bill padding can be avoided. We prefer, of course, to turn the car over at once to a legitimate firm in the towing-and-repair business."

Still another report hit at what were called "tow-car racket cops." It revealed: ". . . numerous instances of threats against motorists who wanted to call their own insurance companies. These threats were made by police officers at the scene. They demanded that one of their pet firms be used. They threatened to issue a ticket charging a violation which would make it appear the motorist was at fault in the accident."

And further: "We [insurance companies] have had to submit to these tactics. A jury can be swayed by a policeman's testimony, resulting in a costly verdict against us."

Another investigator reported: "The tow-car operators have an efficient scouting system. They learn quickly, often with police connivance, of accidents, the whereabouts of the driver and car.

"A scout will track down the dazed, often injured, motorist. The driver is persuaded to sign a form giving the garage blanket authority to take possession of the car and do the repairs.

"Knowing the reputation of some firms, we have

warned motorists not to authorize repairs. But then the garage will demand a hundred dollars for the release of the car being held.

"And," he concluded, "that is only a little of what we've been up against."

In Philadelphia a few years ago, insurance investigators found seven garages involved in what was described as "an auto-repair snatching racket." "In many cases, accident victims signed authorization to have their cars removed even before the ambulance arrived," an investigator disclosed.

The District Attorney moved in, found that tow-car companies actually used "salesmen" to cruise the city, listening to police radio bulletins, ready to speed to the scene of any accident. Said one report: "The main object is to be first at the scene. The next step is to get the victim to sign a form giving the repair shop the power of attorney. Sometimes we had to get new forms signed because the first were too blood-spattered to be legible."

Washington, D.C., too, has been plagued with crooked tow-car operators. An investigation there found that ambulance chasers, equipped with special police-radio receivers, descended upon the scene of every major accident, breaking speed limits to get there and charging the motorist an exorbitant fee to tow his car even a few blocks.

Recently, a motorist was charged twenty-five dollars to have his car towed a distance of just four blocks! In another accident, a motorist asked the tow-truck operator to move his car to a garage with a nearby branch office. Rather than tow the vehicle to the nearby northeast garage, the tow-truck operator hauled it to the Bethesda branch—ten miles from the scene of the accident. Charge for this service: $46.10.

As a result of AAA complaints to Washington's District Board of Commissioners, a regulation was finally passed by the Board in April, 1965, with these provisions:

- All tow-car operators must be licensed.

- Tow-car operators are prohibited from using short-wave radios tuned to the metropolitan police force frequency.

- Tow-car operators are not permitted to obtain signed statements from car owners involved in accidents, agreeing that thte tow-car company's garage will handle repairs.

For motorists traveling through the Rocky mountains, an engine breakdown can mean real trouble. Says the Rocky Mountain Motor Club of Denver:

"One abuse we've found is the towing of accident-damaged vehicles that are still driveable. A tow-truck will hook onto a car before any check is made to see if it can be moved under its own power—for instance, by merely bending a fender slightly to free a wheel. But few motorists carry crowbars or equipment necessary to do this easy job."

One suburban Denver tow-truck operator considered a certain mountain canyon highway his "private territory." Another tow-truck driver, called to that area by an AAA member, was challenged by the tow-truck operator who claimed jurisdiction over the damaged car. Only the intervention of a state patrolman averted a free-for-all.

In Colorado, as elsewhere across the country, the motorist (or his insurance company or auto club) pays not just for one tow, but for two, plus storage charges to boot. For example, if an accident occurs in the evening and the repair establishment is closed, the towing firm first hauls the damaged vehicle to the towing firm's lot. The car is stored overnight. The next day, it is towed to the garage where the actual repairs are made. Thus, the motorist is hit with a number of charges.

On a fifty-mile desert stretch between Bakersfield, California, and Las Vegas, Nevada, cars break down by the score during hot weather—with the temperature reaching 135 degrees, engines suffer burst water hoses, vapor-lock, and split radiator seams. Countless drivers have been the victims of roving tow-trucks whose operators persuaded them they needed to be towed all the way to Las Vegas. There are, in fact, local garages close at hand all along the way that can readily handle these breakdowns.

In New York City, a 1961 series of articles in the *New York Journal-American* touched off a probe conducted by District Attorneys' offices in four of the city's boroughs. The investigation indicated that motorists were being bilked of more than $10,000,000 a year by auto-towing and repair racketeers. The conspiracy involved conniving cops, lawyers, and top city officials. Here are some things discovered through the probe:

- Tow-car drivers charged that, in many instances, they could not remove a wrecked car from the streets without paying off the police.

- The payoffs ranged from $30 to $50 per car and totalled as much as $3,000,000 a year.

- Some policemen received as much as $75 per car. They qualified for this higher payoff by phoning a favorite tow-car driver to tip him off to an accident, thus enabling him to arrive first at the scene.

- In many cases, garages padded repair bills to cover payoffs and even *deliberately damaged* cars so as to boost the total bill.

The exposé spotlighted a motley cast of characters who fed on the racket:

- A police inspector who could "fix anything" for tow-car drivers "if the price was right."

- A driving school which sold phony chauffeurs' licenses to tow-car drivers unable to get legitimate permits because of police records or a long string of traffic violations. These "licenses" cost $75.

- A Manhattan electronics company that supplied tow-car drivers with police radios for $125. This was in defiance of city and federal laws prohibiting interception of police messages.

- An ambulance-chasing lawyer who later graduated to a high city post. A tow-car operator charged that this official paid him $15,000 over a two-year period.

According to James D. Horan, Assistant Managing Editor of the *New York Journal-American* and director of the newspaper's investigation, "What we uncovered on the tow-car scandal resulted in one of the largest shake-ups in the history of the New York City Police Department. We obtained a payoff book which listed payments to scores of cops. There was even a Sergeants Club, made up only of police sergeants. Their names were listed on the payoff books of local tow-car operators, and they received fees of from five to twenty dollars for every accident tip."

"Has anything changed?" Horan was asked recently.

"I doubt it," he replied. "When the heat is on, the crooks lie low for a bit. But then when things cool off, they take right off again."

Young Sam Crowther, Jr., who lives with his parents in a small town in northern New Jersey, saved $850 as the down payment on a new $3,000 GTO Pontiac convertible. When the car was delivered, he was the envy of the neighborhood's young crowd.

Coming home from work one night, Sam, Jr. parked his car, as he usually did, right outside the house. Watching television after dinner, he heard what he described as a "crashing thump."

"I ran out and there was my car on the sidewalk. Another car had smashed into the rear and was locked on to it. The driver was just sitting there. I went over and found he was blind drunk. Then I saw he was bleeding, so I ran into the house and called the police."

A few minutes later an ambulance arrived with a police car. The attendant said, "He's not hurt bad. Just needs a night's sleep to sober him up. We'll take him to the hospital and check him out."

As the drunk was being helped to the ambulance, a police officer walked over to Sam and asked: "What do you want to do about the car? Have it pulled back into the street, or towed away?"

"Maybe I can drive it," Sam said.

"No, don't try," the officer told him. "If you drive it the way it is, you might not collect full payment."

(This was the first false statement made by the police officer. According to the Insurance Information Institute, driving a car after an accident will in no way affect settlement of an insurance claim.)

Sam, Jr. went on with his story:

"I said I wanted to have it towed away. Then the cop said, 'Do you have your own wrecker or shall we call ours?' I thought he was talking about a police department wrecker so I told him to go ahead and make the call. I asked him where the car would be taken and he told me it would be towed to a body shop he recommended."

A few minutes later the wrecker arrived and the boy watched his pride-and-joy towed away.

Then he asked the officer if the drunken driver would be arrested. "I'm going to the hospital now," the policeman said. "I'll have a talk with him. Probably give him a ticket for reckless driving. But I won't arrest him. It would be difficult to get a doctor to say he's drunk, because he's also injured. And it might cause trouble with your insurance company."

(This was still another false statement. When the Insurance Information Institute was queried on the point, a spokesman said: "We do not know what motivated the officer to say such a thing, but it is completely erroneous. A liability policy remains in effect regardless of the circumstances of the accident or the condition of the driver of the car.")

Two days later, the boy's mother visited the body shop. The owner was most sympathetic. He showed her the car parked beside several others which had been involved in accidents. Obviously this had been a good week for business.

"It's very, very bad," the shop owner said, shaking his head. "The frame is sprung, and I don't know what other trouble we're going to find. But here is an estimate."

He handed Mrs. Crowther an estimate sheet, with items that took up an entire page. At the bottom the total read: $1,095.25.

Sam's father returned that evening from an out of town trip and learned for the first time what had happened. The repair estimate, he knew, was ridiculous. The only thing to do was have the car pulled out of that garage immediately and taken back to the dealer for repairs.

And that's what was done. It cost $42.75 to regain possession of the car from the cop's recommended body shop—a price which included the cost of towing the car from the scene of the accident, storage at $2 per day and something listed as "damage appraisal" in the amount of $20.

The dealer repaired the car and it looked like new for $335 less than the body shop operator had estimated.

What can the average motorist do to protect himself from the tow-car racket? Says Morgan Woods, of the American Insurance Association:

"If you have been directed by the investigating police officer to remove your wrecked car, call your own garage if that's possible. If it's not, and a tow-car on the scene solicits your business, do not sign any form without satisfying yourself that it merely authorizes removal of the car to a place designated by you. Make sure it is *not* an authorization to *repair*. Get a business card from the tow-car operator and find out the towing charge. If you don't do these things and you become a victim, your only recourse is to file complaints with the local Police Department, the prosecutor and the Better Business Bureau. *Don't take it lying down!*"

CHAPTER X

No warning—go slow

THE LITTLE TOWN suddenly loomed up out of the dazzling Alabama sunlight. Frank McKay, a Connecticut school teacher, was driving south to pick up his wife, who had been visiting relatives for the past month. He slowed his car and started through town. Just ahead, a trailer truck was double-parked. McKay swung wide and kept going. The next thing he knew, a police car had screeched up alongside. The officer was motioning for him to pull over.

"What did I do?" McKay asked.

"You crossed a double-line," the officer snapped.

"But I didn't see any double-line," McKay insisted.

"Look again, buddy," was the answer.

The school teacher did. There was a line—but faded almost beyond detection.

The policeman ordered McKay to follow him and they drove to a luncheonette just down the street. The officer motioned McKay to step inside.

"I got to find the judge. You stay here."

The officer started out, then turned back, looked McKay over, and added: "While you're waiting, maybe you'd like a little action." He led McKay to a room in the back of the luncheonette. Five men were kneeling around a blanket—the "action" was a crap game, going full blast.

"Join in," said one of the men.

"I don't know anything about dice," McKay protested.

"We'll show you," the man responded. "It's simple. You shake 'em and roll 'em out. And just to prove that we're nice and friendly, the first roll is on the house."

McKay took the dice that were pressed into his hand and threw. Two ones came up.

"Snake-eye," the man said. "You lose. But it didn't cost you anything. Now put down five dollars and shoot again."

McKay knew he had no choice. The arresting officer was part of the plot. He placed a five-dollar bill on the blanket and threw the dice. A five came up. His point. It was eight on the next roll, then four; on the fifth pass it was seven.

"You crapped out," he was told.

And so began Frank McKay's education in the fine art of "traffic traps" set to plague the American motorist. It proved to be an expensive course. An hour later, when McKay was allowed to stop and take inventory, he found he had lost $185.

At this point, the police officer mysteriously reappeared and announced: "Can't find the judge—must have gone visiting. No knowing when he'll get back. So I guess I'll have to let you go."

That happened only a year ago, the American Automobile Association told us at headquarters in Washington, D.C.

The use of speed traps to fleece motorists is widespread, though the gambling bit is a new gimmick. There are few states which don't use some variation of the basic racket to generate income by taking unfair advantage of out-of-state motorists.

The American Automobile Association lumps it under its own term of "Very Strict Enforcement." Says Cornelius R. ("Hap") Gray, director of the AAA's legal department: "Our current files are jammed with complaints from motorists who have been arrested as a result of 'strict enforcement policy' on the part of the police and local authorities.

"We worked hard to get rid of speed traps," Mr. Gray explained recently. "These were situations in which drivers were actually trapped into breaking the law. But they've come up with new gambits. It's the old 'soak-the-motorist' policy with a new look."

Here are the results of an on-the-spot investigation based on affidavits in the files of some 250 AAA clubs around the country. The number of "Strict Enforcement" areas is updated from time to time. Often there are as many as 40 such locations on the list.

A prime one is in Georgia, on U.S. Route 301—the fastest and most direct route from the Greater New York Metropolitan Area to the Florida vacation lands. Motorists had complained for years of speed traps. Things got so bad that Georgia's Governor Carl Sanders finally set up a Speed Trap Board. It didn't take the Board long to zero in on their target—Long County Sheriff Wayne McCord Jones. The roof fell in on Jones after he provided the following testimony to the Board:

QUESTION (from a Board member): "When a motorist is arrested and fined, who gets the money?"

ANSWER (by Jones): "Well, we have the fee system. It's divided between myself, the justices of the peace, and the County."

Q. "Why have there been so many arrests?"

A. "To protect public safety and to make revenue for my office."

Q. "What is the prime consideration?"

A. "Safety. But I don't object to the take-home pay either. We've all got to get along, you know."

Q. "What would happen if you were off the fee system?"

A. "I would not make as many arrests."

Governor Sanders promptly removed all enforcement of traffic laws from the responsibility of Sheriff Wayne McCord Jones and placed it in the hands of the State Public Safety Department.

In November 1965, the Sheriff was indicted for income tax evasion. The Government charged that he had filed fraudulent returns, claiming an income of $1,815 when, according to the Government, he and his wife actually owed $10,821 in taxes! This was ex-Sheriff Jones' reaction:

"It's all because of complaints from half-breeds and wops. They go up north and say Georgia doesn't know how to run its courts—from the Governor on down."

The strictest of all "strict enforcement" towns along Route 301 has been Ludowici, Georgia, which had the deserved reputation of being the country's most notorious speed trap. There a traffic light, deliberately rigged by the police and set at a key intersection (where motorists barely had time to realize they were near a town) could be made to flash green for only a few seconds. Thousands of motorists were arrested at the spot. Then in 1960, local merchants and motel owners, who realized they were losing business, got together and put up money for a new light that worked—without interference—properly. Conditions improved for a while.

But the local authorities, who received a percentage of each fine collected, switched to other techniques for snaring the unsuspecting motorist. South of the light, as a driver heads out of town, he comes onto a stretch of four-lane highway. The natural instinct is to return to the 60 mph highway speed. Most do—and many are arrested. The explanation is that the stretch of highway is still technically in Ludowici—and the speed limit, though not posted, is still 35 mph.

Another notable trap is in the tiny community of Horseshoe Bend, Idaho. In past years, the town has virtually lived on the fines paid by out-of-town motorists. Here is what one victim reported:

"I was coming down the hill into Horseshoe when this officer stopped me. I had been doing 30 mph, but he said I was going 45 mph in a 35 mph zone. He didn't look at all like one of the frontier marshals you see on television. He was shabbily dressed. All he had was a badge. He directed me to a house where the justice of the peace lived. It turned out to be a woman. She yelled at us to come in when he knocked. She said, 'Do you plead guilty or not guilty?' She quickly added that if I pleaded not guilty I would have to stay in her home for a few days until the trial came up. If I pleaded guilty, she said, the fine would be $18. After I figured what it would cost me to stay over, I paid the $18 and was on my way."

Another Horseshoe Bend victim told almost the same story: "I had just left a 15 mph zone and passed a slow-moving pickup at a speed of about 25 mph. The next thing I knew, an officer stopped me and said I had crossed the white line and was guilty of reckless driving. He told me to appear in court in five days. Being a working man, I decided to plead guilty so I wouldn't lose time from my job. I felt I was being taken, but what could I do? I was over a barrel and in no position to spend a lot of time and money fighting the case. I was told by the justice of the peace that I could get as much as five days in jail and suspension of my license for 30 days for reckless driving. So I pleaded guilty and paid a fine of $25 plus $3 court costs."

(Investigation of cases similar to this shows that the fine is usually split: $10 to the justice of the peace, $6 to the arresting officer, and the balance to the county.)

The complaints along Route 66 fill a number of large folders in the AAA's Washington, D.C., headquarters. Most of the complaints concern the town of Grants, New Mexico, just east of Albuquerque. Though difficult to find on the map, the area is well remembered by motorists who've been there. Within Grants is a no-passing zone, marked by a faded yellow line. An officer stationed there full-time manages to hand out an average of 180 tickets a month, despite the pleas of drivers who insist they didn't see the line. It is not unusual for the officer to wave down as many as three motorists at a time. Almost all arrests involve out-of-town or out-of-state motorists. The local justice of the peace, John V. Horacek, is bitterly angry with the AAA for having put Grants on its "Very Strict Enforcement" list. "People are prejudiced before they even enter a traffic court here," says Horacek. Asked why something was not done to mark the "no-passing" zone clearly, he replies, "That's not my responsibility. The State Highway people should take care of that."

Budville, New Mexico, is another town which has

used a faded yellow line to fill the town coffers. Justice of the Peace Jesse L. Ross also blames the town's bad reputation on the AAA. "That big-money outfit has made motorists abusive. One California woman called me a cornball. I fined her $28.50. They walk in and say they're going to report me. I say, 'Go right ahead.' They complain that I'm on a commission basis and split the fee with the arresting officer. 'So what,' I say. 'You still get a fair trial.' That's the kind of headaches I have."

Don't feel too sorry for J. L. Ross. He has managed to do very well despite the "headaches." Adjoining his court is his trading post, a restaurant and bar, where motorists usually head to relax after having a taste of Budville justice.

Another New Mexico booby-trap has been Milan. Authorities blame Civil Rights, as well as the AAA, for its reputation. Involved is a 45 mph zone. Obey it and you cause a traffic jam. The Police Magistrate, T. D. Davenport, sits in his office just off the highway, comfortable in a well-holstered lounger, waiting for business.

"Everybody is speeding," he says. "But my real trouble is those Negroes from out-of-state with their big cars. When they come into court the first thing they say is that I'm prejudiced. Why I've had as many as four or five a day tell me the same thing. But I definitely am not prejudiced. They get hit with the same fines as the whites."

New Mexico is not to blame for all of the complaints involving Route 66. The neighboring state of Arizona has its share. One motorist from New York City was arrested in Bowie (pop. 550) and charged with driving 90 mph—despite the fact that he had a governor on the motor of his car which prevented his doing more than 60 mph. Here is his story:

"I explained to the justice of the peace why I couldn't be doing 90 mph. I even said I was willing to have my car tested to prove it. He told me, 'That wouldn't mean anything . . . you had a *tailwind.*' He fined me $25 and said I was getting a break because that was less than $1 a mile."

Adjoining Bowie is Winslow, which has bred gripes, too. "The officer stopped me and said I was violating Section 28-725 of the Arizona Revised Statutes," a Chicago motorist complained to the AAA. "He said I crossed a white line, but there was no white line at that point. I even went back later and double checked. The justice of the peace advised me to plead guilty—or come back in 10 days for trial. What choice did I have? I pleaded guilty and accepted a $15 fine." (This particular motorist had been driving for 20 years and held a highway safety citation from the Secretary of State of Illinois. But that didn't make any difference in Winslow, Arizona.)

The state of Arkansas, noted for its cabbage, is just as notable for the cabbage that some of its towns extract from motorists. The leading offender used to be Morrilton, just west of Little Rock, on a main highway through the state. It has a lucrative tourist attraction: it is the gateway to Winthrop Rockefeller's sprawling million-dollar ranch atop Petit Jean Mountain. The city fathers had a supplemental source of revenue—"speeders." Complaint after complaint poured into AAA offices. Motorists began to avoid the town and Morrilton started losing business.

This put the City Council and Mayor Thomas H. Hickey, in particular, in a spot. His Honor, needing an out, issued a blistering statement to the press which declared that Morrilton had unfairly been put on the "strict enforcement" list because an AAA "big-wig" had been arrested for doing 80 mph in a 60 mph zone. "And that official," Hickey charged, "had the gall to come into my office and ask me to 'fix' the ticket. I, of course, refused."

The Mayor's press conference created quite a storm. Frank M. Potter, general manager of the Arkansas AAA, roared into town ("I intend to take punitive action") and demanded from Hickey the name of the "AAA official" who had asked to have a ticket fixed.

There were several days of silence from His Honor. Finally, Hickey announced that naming the official would "not be our policy." In a subsequent newspaper interview he admitted he didn't know whether the alleged speeder "was an AAA official or not."

Needless to say, Potter didn't alter his judgment of Morrilton. "We'd had complaints for two years about the way they treated motorists. The town stayed on the list until it reformed."

Another Arkansas town turned out to be a lot smarter. This was Ward, about as far east of Little Rock as Morrilton is west. At one time Ward chewed up motorists like a threshing machine. On U.S. 67, as it comes through the town, there were a number of confusing yellow double lines ("no-passing") which brought numerous arrests and subsequent complaints.

"You just don't know which way to go," motorists insisted.

The AAA sent out a warning to its 8,000,000 members around the country. Potter, who had moved in on Morrilton, received a call from Ward's Mayor, its Chamber of Commerce and its police. They wanted help. Potter contacted the State Highway Department and asked them to send an engineer. The Highway Department's engineer made a study which revealed that "the yellow 'no-passing' lines were a hazard and resulted in excessive delay, disobedience and passing maneuvers which increased accident frequency." The town went along with a recommendation that the entire "speed zone" system be changed, and it was. The number of issued tickets dropped off—and so did the accident rate.

The Highway Department summed it up:

"Under normal conditions, 85 out of 100 drivers will drive at a speed which is both reasonable and safe. If speed limits are unreasonably low, they will be ignored. If they are too high, 85 per cent of the drivers will still drive at a safe and reasonable speed."

Then there was this significant conclusion: "These studies have shown that unreasonable speed limits are not observed by the average driver and enforcement becomes an impossibility."

Kentucky, famous for hospitality, doesn't always extend its good-will to motorists. It earned the dubious honor of being "far and wide the worst state in the nation in traffic trapping" after the Louisville Automobile Club investigated complaints about the town of Bonnieville on U.S. 31 W—a major north-south route through the state. Four other towns had already been placed on the AAA's "very high enforcement list." This is what was uncovered in Bonnieville:

It's a town of 500 people. In the past it had had three policemen, three patrol cars and one radar-detection device. Most of the town's income is derived from traffic fines. When the judge was asked to show his record of citations, he refused, although this should be a matter of public record. It developed that there *was* no published record of the finances of Bonnieville, as required by Kentucky law.

Last year a group of Kentucky AAA clubs backed a bill requiring that revenues from traffic fines be paid directly into the state treasury. The bill, a major piece of reform legislation, breezed through the Kentucky Senate, but ran into a log-jam in the House.

Investigation revealed that key legislators had been warned: "Vote against the bill or forget about running in the next election." And that was that. The bill died and Kentucky is still the worst traffic trap in the nation.

But it would be a mistake to believe that all the traffic traps are in small towns. Conditions are just as bad in the big cities. New York, for example, has some beauts. The lid was blown off by—of all persons—a traffic court judge. He is Criminal Courts Judge Edward D. Caiazzo, known as the toughest judge in the city of traffic violators (he once hit a scofflaw with 485 days in jail). Women defendants who appear before him in slacks make him see red. He told one: "You look like you're dressed for the bedroom—not a courtroom. Go home and come back properly attired."

New York City motorists couldn't have been more surprised when Judge Caiazzo suddenly emerged in a new light as their champion. It all came about when a busy street in Staten Island was made a one-way street overnight as a result of new highway construction. Drivers were caught unaware. Hundreds of tickets were handed out. The judge heard about the problem and decided to take a look. He saw. The next day in court a flock of summonses involving the spot came before him. He freed 25 motorists, with this blistering comment: "The police turned this into a traffic ambush. Patrol cars were attracted [there] . . . Instead of directing traffic, the police handed out summonses. Why, one radio car could have helped these confused motorists."

Then Caiazzo looked up and out over the crowded courtroom. "The job of the police," he declared, "is to help motorists instead of harassing them."

Another New York driver trap got its come-uppance from Traffic Commissioner Henry A. Barnes. It involved an intersection at Broome and Sullivan Streets. As the motorist drives west on Broome, he reaches Sullivan, which is one-way going north. But this is a "play street," which means that cars are prohibited. The only indication of the restriction was a small, faded and battered sign which usually sat in the gutter. The cops carefully refrained from putting in a request that the sign be replaced. It was all very convenient for the Fourth Precinct which—like all other police precincts in the city—is responsible for issuing a specific quota of tickets. An officer was regularly assigned to the play street two or three mornings a week; through his vigilance, 125 to 150 tickets a month were issued. When the situation finally came to the attention of Commissioner Barnes, he ordered an investigation. As a result, the old sign was scrapped and a new one installed. Since then, the Fourth Precinct has had to look elsewhere to fill its traffic ticket quota.

Commissioner Barnes expressed his views on motorist traps succinctly and well: "Traffic rules and regulations for our streets and highways are vital and necessary. They should and must be enforced. *But it is wrong when they are regarded primarily as a source of revenue*—rather than in the light of their prime purpose, which is to promote safety, deter accidents, and expedite the movement of traffic."

How can *you* avoid getting trapped?

1. Watch for any sudden change in posted speed signs.

2. In passing through any small town, be on the alert for double lines which may be faded or partially hidden.

3. At intersections, watch for traffic lights which

may have been placed, either deliberately or by accident, in such a way as to make it difficult for the motorist to see if he has a green signal.

And if you are a victim of a speed trap? "Squawk," says Russell E. Singer, formerly executive vice-president of the AAA. "Make some noise. Tell the newspapers about it. Write the Mayor, the Governor and, in particular, your local AAA club. You don't have to be a member. Present an affidavit of what happened and a copy of the receipt for the fine or the bail."

Singer paused and leaned back in his chair in his Washington office. "Remember," he told us, "it's an old American custom to beef about injustices . . . and it still works."

CHAPTER XI

Justice of the purse

"In many towns and communities in twenty-five of our states, the justices of the peace only get paid when the verdict is guilty after a motorist is charged with a traffic violation. This is a clear violation of the due process clause of the Constitution of the United States."— From a statement by a member of the American Bar Association.

The old upright was taking a beating as the piano player pounded out the blues. But the regulars, gathered at the bar, were more interested in the coin-operated bowling game. It lit up like a Christmas tree as the local pool-hall hustler made his day's pay—12 strikes in a row for a perfect 300. The joint applauded.

The scene was Gross' Bar in the town of Goodfellow Terrace, Missouri, a community of 800 on the outskirts of St. Louis. Gross' Bar resembled any tavern you might see from one coast to the other, with one difference: the bar also served fines. It was the local Court of Justice. Regularly, over the years, a city judge sat in the rear of the saloon and held court. The drinking customer got a break—every fourth drink on the house. The motorists accused of traffic violations were not as fortunate.

One March afternoon, Mrs. Katie Johnson, a stenographer from the nearby town of Clayton, was stopped inside the village limits by a uniformed police officer.

"You were doing thirty miles an hour in a twenty-mile-an-hour zone," he told her.

"But officer," she protested, "I didn't see any sign."

"Ignorance is no excuse," he snapped. "You're guilty. The fine is ten dollars," and with that handed her an addressed envelope rubber-stamped: "Goodfellow Police Department, 4223 Rosewood Avenue." (This later proved to be the home address of City Marshal Martin M. Burns, the town traffic fine collector.)

"Just put your money in the envelope," the officer advised Mrs. Johnson. "It'll save going to court."

For years in Goodfellow Terrace, the practice had been to pay and forget. But this time, local justice had run into a stubborn woman.

"If I'm guilty, let the court decide," Mrs. Johnson declared.

The officer was annoyed. "Okay, lady, you're under arrest. I'm taking you in."

The "court," of course, was Gross' Bar. At the big sign "Beer," the officer waved her to a halt.

"I'm not going in," she announced. "I'm a Baptist. I've never been in a tavern in my life, and I'm not starting now."

Katie Johnson stood her ground. She wouldn't enter the bar despite the insistence of the officer. A king-sized commotion was soon on view outside the "courtroom." The officer was threatening to arrest her when Edward T. Wright, a young attorney who was mayor of nearby Brentwood, arrived. He had been summoned to the scene by a local newspaperwoman. Wright, after hearing the case, offered his professional services without fee. "I felt it was about time someone made a test case of the town's barroom justice," he recalled.

Wright entered Gross', walked past the customers gathered at the bar and approached the "bench," a wooden table in the rear at which sat Judge Otto Hofele and Town Attorney Robert W. Henry.

"This is a violation of Mrs. Johnson's basic Constitutional rights," Wright was shortly pointing out. "Her religious beliefs prevent her from entering a tavern."

"My suggestion," interrupted Henry, "is for her just to take a plea. That will take care of it."

"She definitely will not plead guilty," retorted Wright. "I need time to prepare my case. I ask for a continuance."

It was granted, and thus began a year-long battle

to achieve justice for Mrs. Johnson. Among the legal moves by Attorney Wright was a petition filed with the Missouri Supreme Court, charging that Judge Hofele was prejudiced. The following testimony, taken from a deposition, was introduced. The questioning is by Attorney Wright, with Judge Hofele testifying.

Q. "Did you ever say that Mrs. Johnson was eccentric?"

A. "Maybe I did. A lot of people are eccentric."

Q. "The case is, did you say 'disgusting'?"

A. "Yes, sir."

Q. "Why do you think that?"

A. "Because it's so minor. I don't see no place for such publicity."

Q. "You seem upset over the case."

A. "I think it's disgusting to make such publicity over the case. I mean it's not worth the time that we are spending on it."

The Municipal Judges Association of St. Louis did not exactly concur with Judge Hofele's attitude. Its Committee on Courtrooms was ordered to make a complete investigation, and as a result, they charged that "Goodfellow Terrace represents a black mark on all municipal courts and is a disgrace to the law." The charge referred also to "the judge and the city attorney sitting at a plain table . . . the defendants passing under a beer sign . . . the noises of the tavern. . . ."

The events shook Goodfellow Terrace as had nothing in its previous history. Today, the town has a new courtroom and a new attorney. The charges against Mrs. Katie Johnson were dismissed.

"It all goes to show," observed lawyer Wright, "what one person with determination can do to clean up a bad situation."

Elsewhere in the country, there aren't many motorists who receive the justice Mrs. Johnson did, primarily because they are not willing to stand up and fight. And few are likely to find someone like Edward Wright to back them up. In twenty-five of our fifty states, thousands of small town "judges" operate in clear violation of the law, growing rich by mulcting motorists.

The information in this chapter comes from the American Bar Association, the AAA, and other official sources. It should serve as an eye-opening for the 2,000,000 car owners who are arrested annually.

In one little New Mexico town, a farm community of slightly over 400 people, the beauty parlor proprietress, a buxom blonde known as Flo, spends a good deal of time dispensing town justice. Flo's gavel is a hairbrush, and the "bench" is littered with jars of cosmetics. Behind it a hair-color chart hangs on the wall. Standing before the bench, in a recent incident, was the town constable and the first defendant of the day, a motorist from St. Louis who was headed west for California until he suddenly found himself in police custody.

"What's the charge?" asked Flo.

"He was doing sixty miles an hour in a thirty-five-mile zone, Your Honor."

"I can't understand all of this," the motorist protested. "I slowed down to thirty-five as I went through town. When I got out of town, I went back to the state highway speed. Why was I stopped?"

Flo fixed her mascaraed eyes on the culprit and said sternly: "The thirty-five mile per hour zone runs three miles in both directions. And I insist that the law be obeyed here."

The man from Missouri tried to debate the matter further, but Flo cut him short. "You can argue at the trial. I'm setting the case down for a week from today. Bail is $50."

"But I'm going to Los Angeles," he pleaded. "It'll be impossible for me to get back here."

"In that case," Flo ruled, "you'll have to plead guilty. The fine is $25, plus $6.20 court costs. And no checks."

To resume his trip westward, the motorist had no choice but to count out thirty-one dollars. And put it all down on the "bench"—between a can of wave-set and a bottle of hair-dye.

The story of Flo and her double career has actually been written up by the local press as a kind of home-town-girl-makes-good feature.

The following information derives from sworn testimony given to the State Legislature by a State Judicial Study Committee set up to probe "the Courts of New Mexico." These verbatim remarks come from justices of the peace who were questioned:

- "It was near the end of the year. So I told the state police not to bring me any more business. All I make now goes to income tax. So I told them to quit enforcing the law."

- "I know a lot of justices of the peace who aren't qualified. They can't even sign their name, and can't even read or write."

- "Yes, the man was shot three times in the heart and once in the head. I ruled it suicide. I felt I wasn't in a position to make an expert opinion."

- "What's wrong is the ignorance of the law. A lot of them don't know or just don't want to follow the statutes."

One justice of the peace was asked about the amount in traffic fees he turned over to the county:

Q. "That last check you gave—was it good?"

A. "The last one was not, no, sir."

Q. "What did it amount to?"

A. "Seven hundred and fourteen dollars."

Q. "Have the county commissioners tried to collect from you since?"

A. "Yes."

Q. "Have they been successful?"

A. "No, sir."

Q. "How much more than the seven hundred and fourteen dollars do you owe?"

A. "I wouldn't exactly know. It runs into a considerable amount."

Another JP was asked:

Q. "How many cases have you handled?"

A. "My records show five hundred and seventy."

Q. "Have you ever dismissed a case brought in by an officer?"

A. "I don't believe I have dismissed a single case."

Still another:

Q. "You are telling us that you are unaware of any laws governing justices of peace since 1953."

A. "That's right."

Q. "Yet you sit there and judge people without knowing exactly what the law is?"

A. "Well, I mean—it's just one of those things."

The report was filed with the New Mexico Legislature in 1961. We asked the office of Governor Jack M. Campbell if things had changed since then. The Governor's press secretary, Maurice E. Trimmer, said, "Unfortunately not. But we're working on a broad program of reform. We want to get away from the fee system for judges."

A few years back, there was a popular song about a mythical town which asked: "How are things in Glocca Morra?" The song supplied no real answers. But if you talk to some of the motorists who have been arrested on traffic charges along Route 99 north of Seattle's city limits, you *will* get answers. They can tell you all about a real-life Glocca Morra—although it is not on most maps.

An official report defines Glocca Morra as an "artificial political division set up to create business for local justices of the peace." One court record involves a motorist tried and convicted there of a traffic violation. He took the case to the State Supreme Court for a change of venue. His contention was: "You can't try me in a justice of the peace court. It's all on the fee system. I can't get a fair trial. There will be prejudice."

The court held against a trial in another jurisdiction on the rather flimsy grounds that "the amount of money involved was not large enough to induce prejudice."

The defendant lost the case, but one jurist who ruled against the majority wrote: "The income of justices of the peace depends directly on the number of cases to be decided. If no case is filed, he receives nothing. *The vice is inherent in the system.*"

A subsequent investigation by the American Bar Association, which has a committee on traffic reform, revealed that over a certain period of time 2,372 traffic-violation charges were presented in Glocca Morra—and *none* in surrounding areas. The police were taking all of their business to Glocca Morra. The fees collected in that one small precinct totaled over $6,000, while neighboring JPs collected nothing. "We are not able to say why the police favored this particular justice of the peace—but we have our suspicions," a Bar Association report stated.

There have been other studies dealing with the situation in the state of Washington. From one recent report: "There is wide fluctuation of income among justices of the peace. Under the current system, they compete with each other for fees." Further along in this official report is the statement: "We have on record the case of one justice who, in a single year, made more in fees than the annual salary of a Supreme Court Justice in the State of Washington."

The Glocca Morra case *has* produced some results. The fee system has been eliminated in three counties: Pierce County (Tacoma), King County (Seattle), and Spokane County (Spokane).

Ohio is known as the "Mother of Presidents," but the state has been far from maternal in its treatment of some of the motorists arrested there on traffic violations. Many municipal and county courts are on the fee system. They have what are known as "Mayor's Courts" in a number of locations—all on the fee system. If a traffic violator is arrested on a through highway, such as the Ohio Turnpike, he is often charged before the Mayor's Court of that town. Along the 240 miles of the Ohio Turnpike, there is one stretch outside Cleveland, just 2.3 miles long, which passes through the town of Boston Heights. Along this 2.3-mile zone, there were 4,345 arrests in a single year! Police would follow a motorist into the jurisdiction of Boston Heights, make their arrest, then radio ahead to the patrol station: "Tell the Mayor we are bringing someone in." And with that the Mayor would hurry over from his place of business near the town of Boston Heights.

"The defendant," an ABA report concludes, "is taken to a small frame building where he awaits the Mayor's arrival. With the Mayor's appearance, court is open, and the defendant is swiftly found guilty." The judge's income, as well as the arresting officer's, depend upon this rapid meting-out of highway "justice."

If the reader thinks Boston Heights is an exception, let him be introduced to Fremont, another town off the Ohio Turnpike which specializes in traffic violations. Although the county had agreed to pay the police department two dollars for each turnpike violator brought in to the bonding station located at the city police department, the local police decided two dollars per head was not enough. They wanted four.

County officials didn't go along with the demand for an increase, but what they did do was declare all-night cab stands and gas stations "official bonding stations." (Naturally, the bond of $10 to $25 is forfeited if the turnpike violator fails to show up in court a week or more later when his case comes to trial. The bonding technique, in place of merely issuing a traffic ticket, protects the town or county against loss of revenue from out-of-state drivers. The motorist pays—one way or another.)

In Wauseon, Ohio, the legal bonding official has been the desk clerk at the Avery Hotel. Motorists can take a room and wait for their trial if they feel inclined to debate the arresting officer's charges. Most, however, prefer to post bail, then drive off and forget about it.

Consider conditions in Florida's Seminole County, where the justice of the peace buys his job. In the town of Sanford, the JPs were taking in a total of $8,500 a year. Since this hardly covered what they were required to pay the town, they managed to have a law passed which corrected the inequity. The law extended their jurisdiction to cover violations up to $100, and broadened the violations against which a $100 fine could be leveled. Where a fine for drunken driving had once been $500, and out of their jurisdiction, it was now a straight $100 offense and in their bailiwick. As a result, fines jumped to $33,000 a year!

Under Florida law, the mayor of a town may act as a judge unless there is a charter which creates a separate court. In some counties, the mayor is paid for his judicial duties on the basis of two dollars per case. But he is paid only when there is a conviction, and when the fine itself is paid. A similar arrangement governs payment to the arresting officer.

In some towns the mayor also receives two dollars for each arrest, but is paid whether he convicts or not. (In the case of an acquittal, the city makes up the two dollars.) Besides the mayor, the clerk of the court, who is also the city clerk, receives fifty cents for each arrest, with the chief of police collecting eight dollars. A special policeman is employed on a part-time basis to assist the chief and, when *he* makes an arrest, is paid a straight eight dollars.

West Virginia has its own variation: all money collected in fines and fees is placed in a special fund from which the justice of the peace is paid a flat salary.

One West Virginia court case involved a defendant who filed a writ of prohibition against a justice of the peace. It contained these details of JP practices: "It is obvious that a justice must convict an appreciable number of cases where fines and costs are collected in order to secure payment of his own fees. Our investigation showed that the sum of $3,574.87 had been deposited with the sheriff from funds collected. Justices had been paid in fees the sum of $3,573.75. This left a balance of $1.22."

In the state of Kentucky, when a defendant was arrested in Pike County, his attorney refused to produce him for trial, on the grounds that: "This is a fee court. My client cannot possibly receive a fair trial here. Unless he loses, members of the court will not be paid."

The justice of the peace overruled the attorney's motion, impaneled a jury and tried the defendant "in absentia." The jury fixed the fine at $20, which was in addition to a $20 bail bond already forfeited.

The attorney appealed the case to a higher court, which ruled: "It is our opinion that no justification exists for a trial under this system. The existing practice is designed and calculated to deprive accused persons of due process of law."

And here is still another Kentucky case:

"In a little town, I was stopped by a state trooper for crossing a solid white line. I was booked and a date set down for trial. I protested because the trial date was near to Christmas and would have been difficult for me to make. The officer politely told me that the justice of the peace would send me a bill. A few days after I arrived home, I received a bill from the justice, who said he had found me guilty and fined me $22. *He instructed that my check be made out directly to him and mailed to his office.*"

What can be done about this "justice" which plagues the American motorist?

"Steps must be taken by lawmakers *now* if people are to receive the basic justice they deserve in traffic courts," says James P. Economos, who has carried the ball for the American Bar Association's reform program. The ABA plan of action calls for state legislatures to implement the effectiveness of the judicial branch of state government in these ways:

- Eliminate the fee system. Its vicious practices now deny to many citizens the due process of law guaranteed under the Fourteenth Amendment to the Constitution.

- Eliminate the present practice of state, county, and local government which requires traffic courts to estimate anticipated revenue from the handling of traffic cases. This sets a money goal they try to meet.

"If such a system were adopted," says Economos, "maybe a motorist, charged with a traffic violation, would have the same rights that a common criminal gets in court."

CHAPTER XII

Car theft, repossessions, fake auctions, and rent-a-car rackets

MOST OF THE PRECEDING CHAPTERS have dealt with flagrantly criminal practices. There are other rackets which, though minor by comparison, should still be called to the attention of car owners.

Keys by mail

You might be interested to learn, for instance, that for an investment of less than $30, you, too, can be a car thief. You need not know how to jump ignitions, but merely where to buy, by mail, master keys which will open virtually any General Motors, Ford, or Chrysler product.

No one actually knows how large a part master keys play in the booming car theft racket. It is, however, big enough to make a U.S. Senator call for a federal law. Sen. Thomas H. Kuchel (R.-Calif.) recently introduced a bill which provides a $5,000 fine and a sentence up to a year in prison for anyone caught sending master car keys through the mail to unauthorized persons.

The Senator was concerned with the "many mail-order firms which are currently advertising master keys for automobiles." He was referring to ads, appearing in automotive magazines and trade publications, addressed to car dealers, locksmiths, garage and parking lot attendants. "You can earn $50 to $60 a week part time," the ads promise, "in the lost car key business."

Here are the current unofficial rates quoted for master keys:

General Motors	$19.95
Ford	$ 5.00
Chrysler	$ 3.00

(We are unable to explain the differences in the quoted prices.)

Only 1,500 key combinations exist for the millions of GM cars now in service. Ford has about 1,000 combinations, while Chrysler has roughly 500. We have all heard reports of one car's key starting another vehicle. There just aren't enough combinations to give each car a unique key. The car manufacturers are caught in the trap of planned design—lock systems for the ignition, door and trunk are designed at least two years before the car itself goes into production.

The master key problem was one of the first inherited by former Police Commissioner Michael J. Murphy of New York when he became head of the National Auto Theft Bureau. This organization, supported by hundreds of insurance agencies, works closely with police departments throughout the nation in recovering stolen cars.

Over *five hundred thousand* cars are stolen every year. It is estimated that by 1970, a *million* cars will be stolen each year, and, based on current averages:

- Total loss will be $872,608,275
- 72,306 of these cars will not be recovered, for a net loss of $67,027,622
- Another 260,702 will be recovered damaged or stripped—a loss of $52,141,000

When the National Auto Theft Bureau came into being, it recognized the threat of mail-order keys, but its original belief that the practice was illegal proved to be wrong. There was no law on the books against mail-order keys. Not a single state, at that time, had a law governing the sales of master keys.

When Joseph Di Carlo, formerly of the New York City License Commission, received complaints about the careless manner in which master car keys were being made available, he sent a group of inspectors to check on the city's 1,406 key-makers. The inspectors posed as auto owners who needed duplicates of master keys.

In hundreds of cases no questions were asked. The inspectors were neither asked for their names or addresses, nor for proof of ownership, a violation of a city ordinance which specifies that licensed locksmiths must enter in a master register the name of every person ordering a master key. Di Carlo leveled fines, ranging from $10 to $25, on 705 keymakers and warned them that their licenses would be suspended or revoked on the next offense. Only such action as Di Carlo's can begin to slow the national rampage of car thefts.

Legislators in a number of states are gradually awakening to the problem, but thus far only Texas and Oregon have done anything about it. Their legislatures have passed laws which make it an offense to sell or offer to sell master keys which can operate the ignition switch of more than one car.

This is a beginning. Similar action should be demanded in all 50 states.

Repossession is nine-tenths of the law

One afternoon in Leonia, New Jersey, recently, Mrs. Carl Lane, a new mother, answered a knock at the door of the Lane apartment.

"I'm from the finance company," said the man who stood there.

"What's the trouble?" the young mother asked.

"You're behind two payments on the car."

"I'm terribly sorry," Mrs. Lane stammered. "We just had a baby and that's so expensive. We're getting caught up. We'll take care of it next week."

"Okay, lady," said the man. Then, politely tipping his hat, he left.

An hour later, Mrs. Lane, carrying her baby in a car-bed, came out to go grocery shopping. The street space regularly occupied by their car was empty. She went back upstairs and called the police.

"I think somebody stole our car," she told the desk Sergeant.

"Give me the make and license number. I'll check it out right away."

The Sergeant called her back: "Lady, your car wasn't stolen. It was repossessed. Contact your finance company."

It took the Lanes an entire week to regain possession of their car. In addition to the two overdue payments, they were required to pay a repossession fee, plus extras. Once the Lanes had their car back, they discovered that the radio was missing. The ashtrays, both front and rear, were jammed with cigarettes, and an empty whiskey bottle was stashed on the rear floor. The repossessors had obviously had quite a weekend.

Car repossessors make it their business to know the license plate numbers of hundreds of cars wanted for repossession by various finance companies. Most cars are easy to locate as the Lane's had been, but the skilled repossessor can spot the plates of a "wanted" vehicle on a highway or in a distant parking lot and he has no compunction about picking it up, whether or not he has to break into the vehicle.

Repossessions without fair warning occur frequently in communities all across the country. Is this legal? Have the owner's property rights been violated?

"We have no idea just how extensive this widespread victimization of the public is," says Assistant District Attorney Francis X. Smith, head of the Queens DA's Rackets Bureau. "The problem we face is that it's all basically legal."

The fee paid for repossession, usually about $45 per car, turns too many practitioners into merciless grabbers. Commented one honest repossessor recently, "We have a commercial code recognized by legitimate firms in twenty-six states, but some operators act like a bunch of goons and give the rest of us a bad name."

Going, going, gone

Often working hand-in-glove with car repossessors are the used-car auction artists. Their activities were exposed in 1963 by the then New York City License Commissioner Bernard J. O'Connell. Involved were auctioneers who sold cars that had either been seized by repossessors or were being held by garage mechanics who had padded repair bills which motorists couldn't afford to pay.

O'Connell ordered the probe after car owners complained that their autos were sold without their knowledge after they disputed repossession or repair charges.

One of the strangest revelations of the investigation was the fact that, time after time, only one "bidder" attended these so-called "auctions"—a friend of the mechanic's or the mechanic himself. The auctions almost always took place at the garage or shop where the confiscated car was held; and it developed that the "bidder" had been able to buy the car for a fraction of its true value.

"They simply bid the amount of the mechanic's lien," one investigator reported, "wiped the debt off their books and owned the car."

One such "auction" involved a 1959 Chevrolet Biscayne, which went for $450—the exact price of the front-end repair work that had just been completed. Yet at the time, that same model was listed at $1,095 on the books of used-car dealers.

In another case, a motorist's car, involved in an accident, was towed to a shop for an estimate on repairs. When the mechanic quoted a price the next day, the motorist insisted it was too high and refused to have the work done. The mechanic then claimed he had already started to make repairs. The car owner demanded the return of his car and the mechanic refused. The dispute went on for a month.

Finally the garage man called in an auctioneer, and an "auction" was held at the garage. The mechanic "bought" the car for the exact amount of the bill, then turned around and sold it for a nice profit.

Just one more example of how the law can be bent to aid the crook and thwart the motorist.

How honest is the rent-a-car business?

In 1962, auto rental agencies did an estimated $250,000,000 volume with about 65,000 cars. Just three years later, the figure had jumped to an estimated $450,-000,000 with some 121,000 cars. (Figures are from the Car and Truck Renting and Leasing Association.)

Suddenly questions are being asked about the ethics of some operators in the field. The entire matter is now being scrutinized by both a sub-committee of the Senate Banking and Currency Committee and the Motor Vehicle Bureau of the State of New York. The latter agency is already in the process of preparing suggested legislation to control car rental honesty.

The big question centers on mileage.

A personal experience is typical of customer complaints. One of the authors recently rented a car in Englewood, New Jersey, for $5.99 a day plus 9 cents a mile.

"The car is fully insured. No matter what happens, you're covered," he was told as he handed over a $20 deposit.

He drove the car to Long Island, where he stayed for five days. Having heard rumors that some rental agencies set their odometers ahead so that they register more than the true mileage, he decided to check the reading of the rented car against another. The comparison was made several times. In all cases, the odometer reading on the rented car was higher than that on the private car, which had first been double-checked over a measured mile.

In one of the tests, the odometer in the rented car read 1.6 miles, while the other car registered 1.3 miles. This meant that the rented car was clocking 23 per cent more mileage!

Driving back to Englewood, he walked into the rental office to settle his account. As the rental car owner started to figure the charges, a station attendant came in with a report.

"The trunk's been damaged," he announced. "Somebody must have hit the rear of the car."

Ridiculous. There had been no accident. A check of the alleged damage revealed a slight mark on the trunk, nothing more.

"We'll have an appraisal made and send you a bill," the owner said.

A week later the bill arrived. It included $31.93 for rental—a total of $51.93 with the $20 deposit. Mileage was listed at 111. This, as tested, was an overcharge of 23 per cent. At the bottom of the bill was this item: "Damage done to trunk by no source reported by you. Therefore you are liable—$58."

A phone call to the station owner elicited this conversation:

CROWTHER: I got your bill and I have a few questions to discuss. First, I checked the odometer while I had the car and found that it was fast.

OWNER: Impossible. They're checked every week by General Motors.

CROWTHER: Are you telling me a General Motors man comes down to your station and checks them?

OWNER: That's correct. He can't be wrong.

(General Motors was later asked whether it checks odometers on rented cars at the station in question. The answer was no.)

CROWTHER: Now, about this charge of $58 for "damage done to trunk." You told me when I rented the car that it was insured no matter what happened.

OWNER: That's right. But you can't tell us who hit you.

CROWTHER: Well, nobody hit me. But the point is that what you are telling me now is that unless I can apprehend a motorist who hit my rented car the insurance is no good. Is that so?

OWNER: We've got to have somebody to sue. We've got to know who did it.

CROWTHER: Then what you told me when I rented the car was false?

OWNER: You didn't understand.

CROWTHER: I do now!

The "fast" odometer which ran the bill up by 23 per cent may seem a small matter, but consider these figures: that car will do an average of 40,000 miles a year, plus 9,200 "padded" miles for added charges of $828 a year (at the 9c per mile rate). If the shyster operator has 10 cars working for him, he can quietly bilk his customers of an extra $8,280 a year without ever having them find out.

Consumers Union estimates that the car renters of this nation are being cheated of close to $8,000,000 a year! This does not include other charges (such as "trunk damage") that may conveniently crop up.

Readers of *Consumer Reports,* the Consumers Union magazine, have written about this racket:

- A New Yorker who rented a Falcon complained: "I was distressed to find that the odometer reading exceeded true road mileage (checked against a measured mile) by more than 10 per cent."

- A reader who had rented a car in Chicago wrote: "The odometer registered considerably more mileage than was actually covered. I checked with a friend who drove the same distance. His car clocked 320 miles while mine clocked 370."

Consumers Union conducted its own investigation, renting 22 cars in Connecticut, Maine, New York, and Pennsylvania. They checked them against the cars of the same year and make. CU found the average rented car in the test over-registered 3.3 per cent. The range went from 1 per cent to an overcharge of 13 per cent in the case of a car rented from an independent operator. (These are the worst offenders.) In the past five years, CU has conducted a number of similar tests, and found that over-registration went from 1 to 14 per cent.

In Miami, the State Division of Standards, responding to Florida complaints, tested 36 rented cars. All but one over-registered.

What are lawmakers doing about the situation? In October, 1962, New York State joined some 40 other states in adopting an amendment to its weights and measures laws. Known as amendment H44, it provides that the error in all commercial measuring devices, if there is an error, must favor the consumer, not the seller.

Odometer over-registration of more than 1 per cent (a margin allowed for worn tires) is prohibited.

Only two of the 22 rentals tested by CU and only one of the 36 checked in Florida met legal requirements. It is clear that H44 *is not being enforced.*

It has been argued that car rental odometers run fast because car manufacturers make them that way. We checked. The Automobile Manufacturers Association admits that odometers are set to over-register from 1 to 5 per cent, but Association spokesmen have been reluctant to explain why. It should be apparent, however, that if an odometer reaches 40,000 miles 5 per cent to 15 per cent sooner, a replacement will be bought 5 per cent to 15 per cent more quickly.

What can the average car renter do? Without absolute proof of fraud, not much. Unless he does what one Consumers Union correspondent did while vacationing in California. This man checked the odometer on four separate turnpike miles and found it off by more than 15 per cent. Citing this fact to the rental agency, he simply deducted 15 per cent from his mileage fee. And the agency accepted the reduction without a complaint.

Part of the answer to this entire recital of automobile swindle is to squawk—loudly. To your local police department, District Attorney, AAA, Better Business Bureau, your Senator and Congressman. Overall racketeering costs you and your fellow motorists more than seven million dollars a year, and that thought alone ought to bring a roar of protest.

The solutions themselves must come through aggressive action on city, state, and federal levels. Courageous, public-spirited leaders must take the first steps toward drafting meaningful legislation.

If we have made you indignant in reading this book, then our purpose has been served. If we have aroused some public servants to action, then the purpose has been doubly served.

Perhaps it is only fitting that we close with a note on the nation's big junk heap, the auto cemetery. That, too, has been the cause for complaints. Nothing is made easy for the car owner, not even killing off his own car.

For years the streets of our town and cities have been cluttered with abandoned cars. In New York, over 20,000 unwanted vehicles are left to die under bridges or along dimly lighted streets. Now the Sanitation Commission has arranged to tow away, free of charge, any unwanted car on a mutually convenient date.

So there is, finally, a final resting place for those

old heaps that have wheezed their last. All you need to do is dial the right number.

Unfortunately, the rest of a car owner's problems can't be solved that easily. But now that you've been forewarned about the great variety of frauds practiced on the car owner, keep this book handy: the next time you're being set up for one of the many forms of highway robbery, you'll know either how to protect yourself or whom to report the racket to. If enough car owners take action, the nation's biggest swindlers will have begun to meet their match.

Index